SINGER + PIANO/GUITAR

VOCAL SHEET MUSIC

POP BALLADS

D0503912

ISBN 978-1-5400-1511-2

HAL•LEONARD®

Visit Hal Leonard Online at
www.halleonard.com

Contact Us:
Hal Leonard
7777 West Bluemound Road
Milwaukee, WI 53213
Email: info@halleonard.com

In Europe contact:
Hal Leonard Europe Limited
42 Wigmore Street
Marylebone, London, W1U 2RN
Email: info@halleonardeurope.com

In Australia contact:
Hal Leonard Australia Pty. Ltd.
4 Lentara Court
Cheltenham, Victoria, 3192 Australia
Email: info@halleonard.com.au

10 **Angel**
SARAH McLACHLAN

3 **Bridge Over Troubled Water**
SIMON & GARFUNKEL

16 **Can't Help Falling in Love**
ELVIS PRESLEY

22 **Careless Whisper**
WHAM! FEATURING
GEORGE MICHAEL

34 **Ebony and Ivory**
PAUL McCARTNEY
WITH STEVIE WONDER

29 **(Everything I Do) I Do It for You**
BRYAN ADAMS

40 **Faithfully**
JOURNEY

46 **Glory of Love**
PETER CETERA

58 **Hard to Say I'm Sorry**
CHICAGO

53 **Hello**
LIONEL RICHIE

64 **Here and Now**
LUTHER VANDROSS

71 **Hero**
ENRIQUE IGLESIAS

78 **Hey Jude**
THE BEATLES

92 **How Am I Supposed to Live Without You**
MICHAEL BOLTON

87 **I Honestly Love You**
OLIVIA NEWTON-JOHN

98 **I Just Can't Stop Loving You**
MICHAEL JACKSON

103 **I Knew I Loved You**
SAVAGE GARDEN

108 **Just the Way You Are**
BILLY JOEL

119 **Killing Me Softly with His Song**
ROBERTA FLACK

124 **Kiss from a Rose**
SEAL

133 **My Heart Will Go On (Love Theme from 'Titanic')**
CELINE DION

142 **Rainy Days and Mondays**
THE CARPENTERS

147 **Right Here Waiting**
RICHARD MARX

152 **Save the Best for Last**
VANESSA WILLIAMS

162 **Saving All My Love for You**
WHITNEY HOUSTON

157 **Shape of My Heart**
STING

168 **So Far Away**
CAROLE KING

178 **Take My Breath Away (Love Theme)**
BERLIN

173 **Time After Time**
CYNDI LAUPER

184 **Tiny Dancer**
ELTON JOHN

196 **Un-Break My Heart**
TONI BRAXTON

191 **Up Where We Belong**
JOE COCKER &
JENNIFER WARNES

204 **Wonderful Tonight**
ERIC CLAPTON

BRIDGE OVER TROUBLED WATER

Words and Music by
PAUL SIMON

5

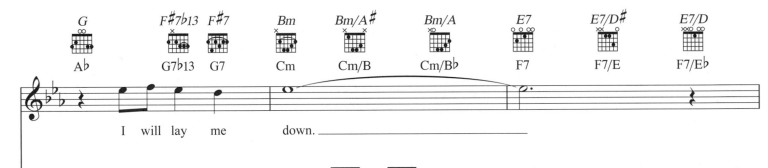

When you're

CODA

trou - bled   wa - ter

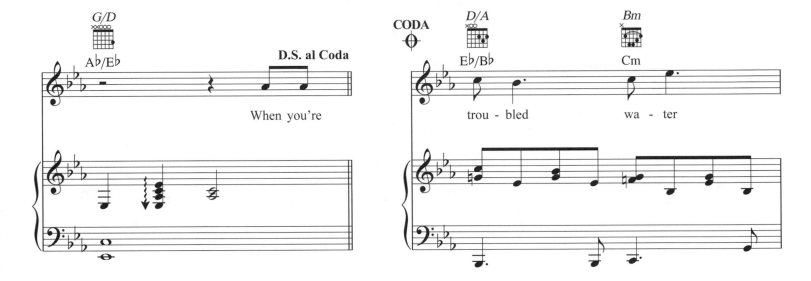

I will lay me   down. _____

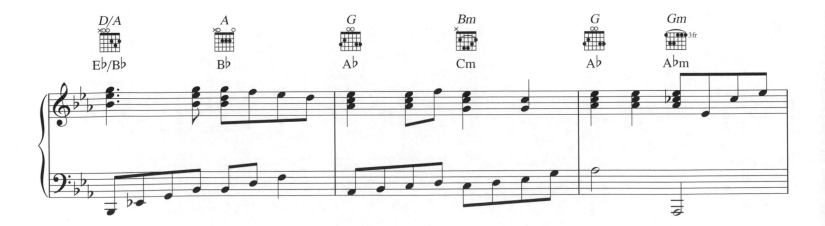

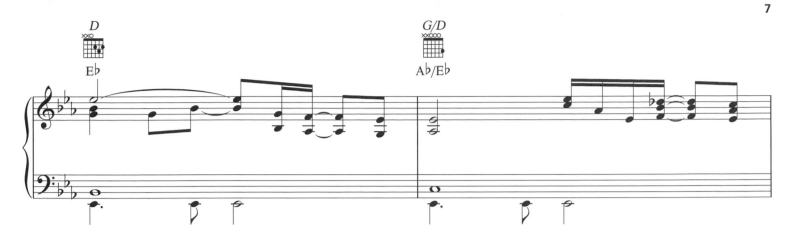

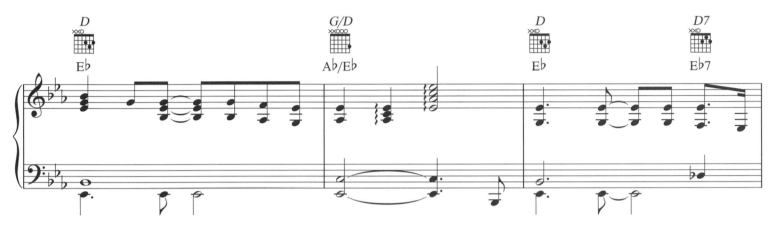

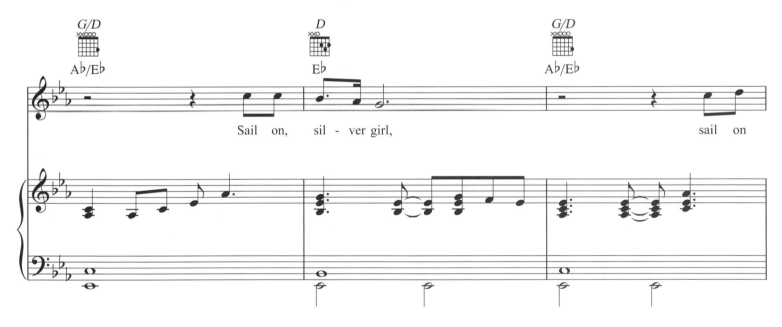

Sail on, sil - ver girl, sail on

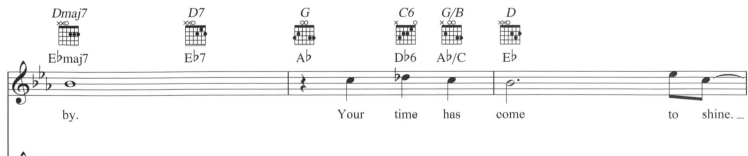

by. Your time has come to shine.

ANGEL

Words and Music by
SARAH McLACHLAN

an - gel. May you find

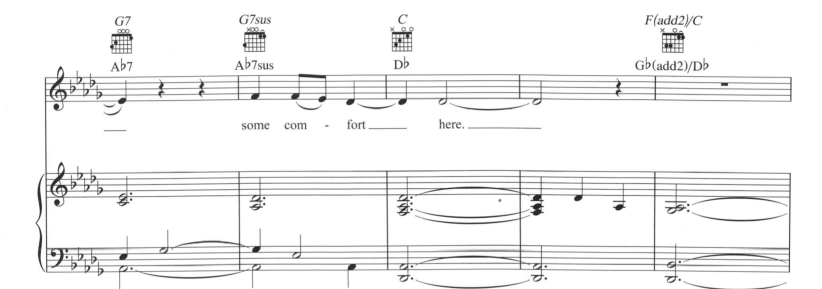

some com - fort here.

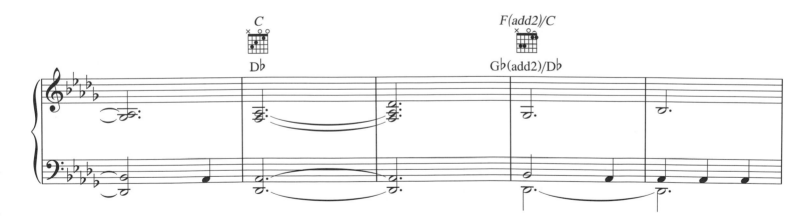

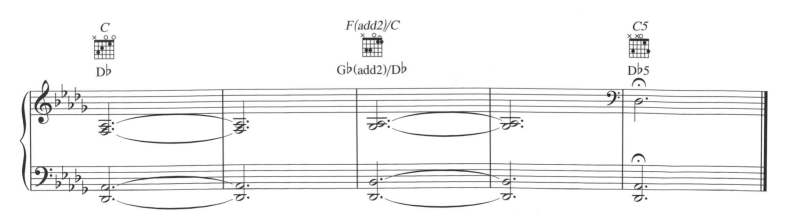

CAN'T HELP FALLING IN LOVE

Words and Music by GEORGE DAVID WEISS,
HUGO PERETTI and LUIGI CREATORE

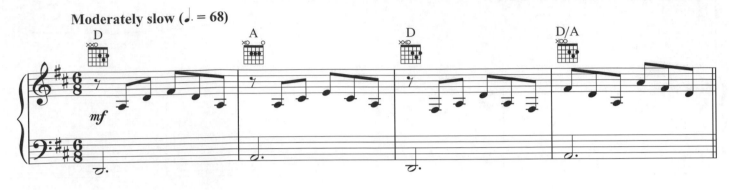

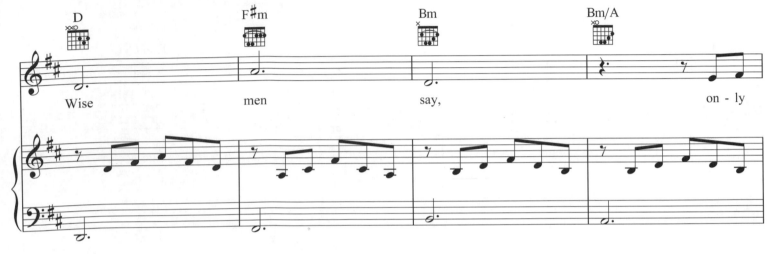

Wise   men   say,   on - ly

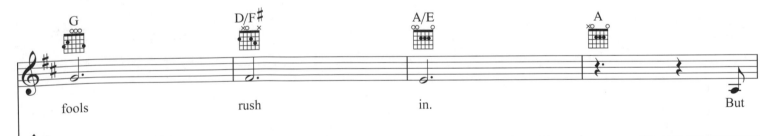

fools   rush   in.   But

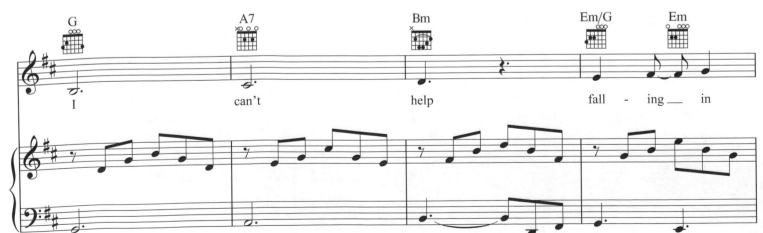

I   can't   help   fall - ing __ in

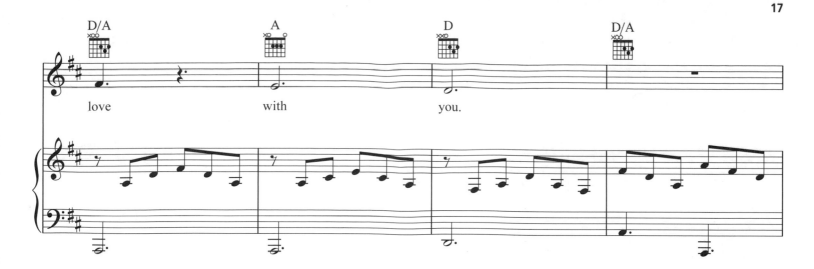

love   with   you.

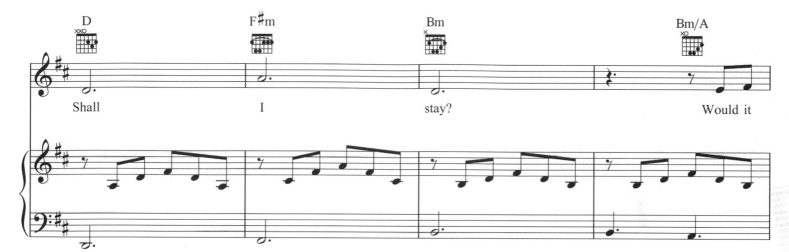

Shall   I   stay?   Would it

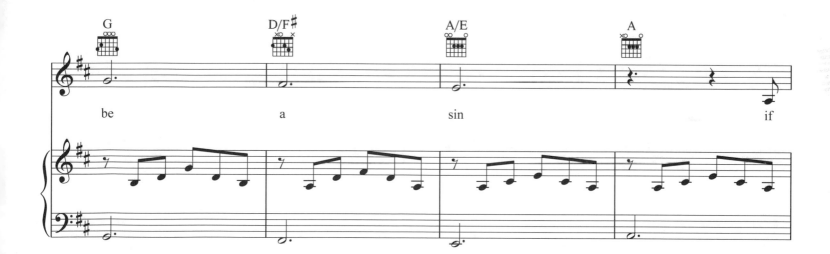

be   a   sin   if

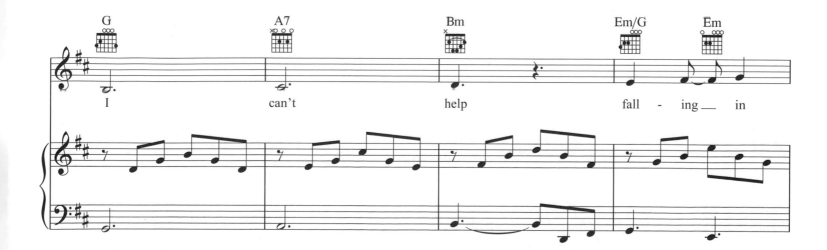

I   can't   help   fall - ing __ in

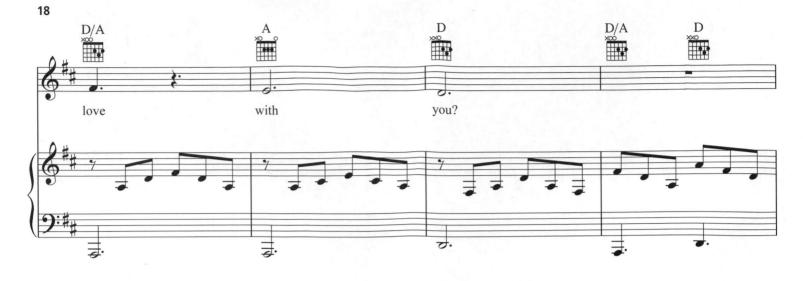

love   with   you?

Like   a ___ riv - er   flows, _____   sure - ly ___ to the sea. _____

Dar - ling, _ so it   goes. _____   Some   things _   are ___ meant to

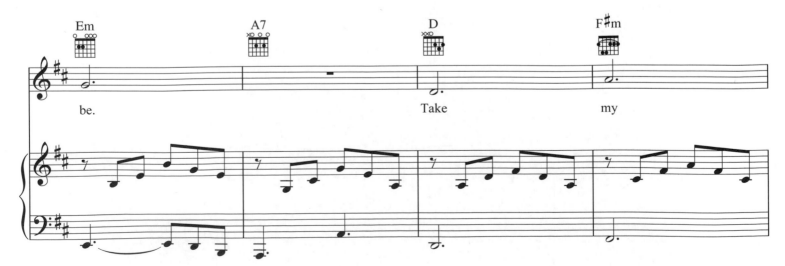

be.   Take   my

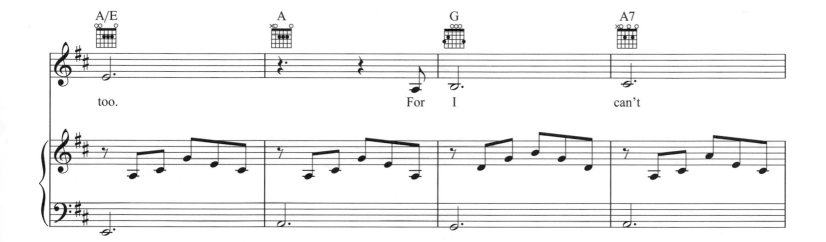

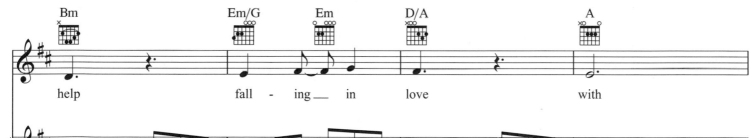

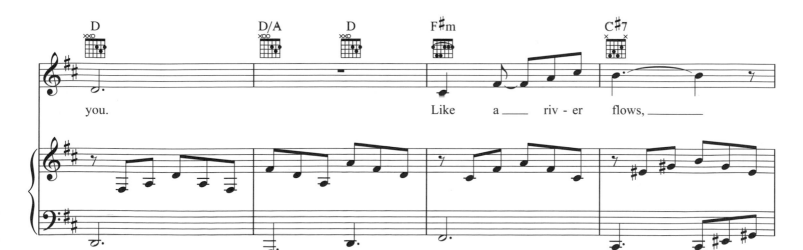

sure - ly to the sea. Dar - ling, so it goes.

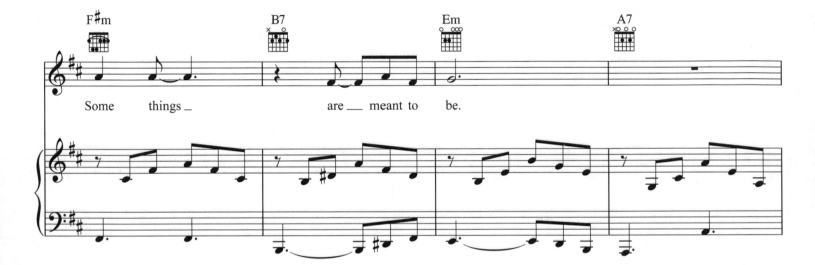

Some things are meant to be.

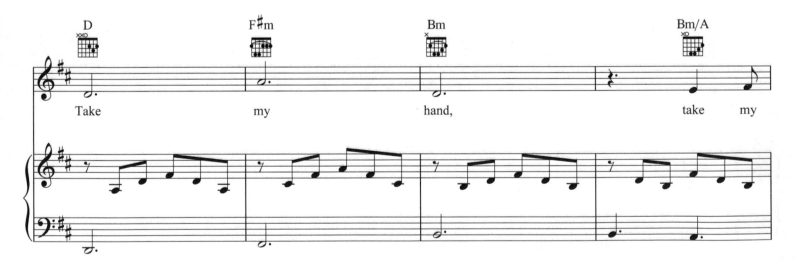

Take my hand, take my

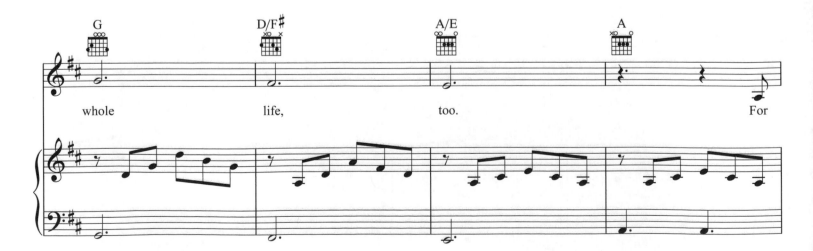

whole life, too. For

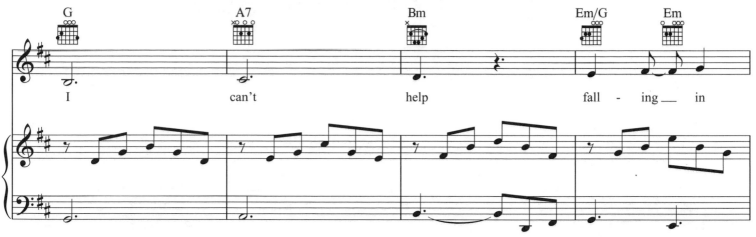

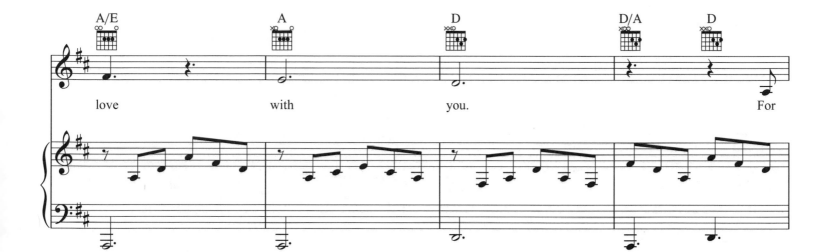

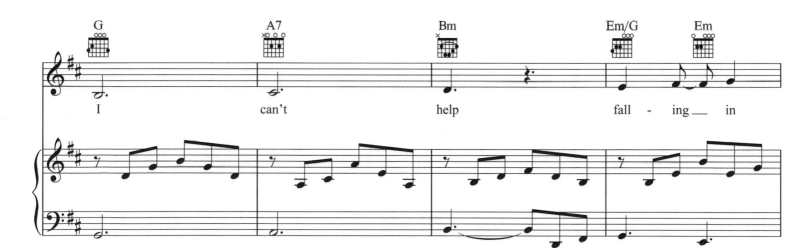

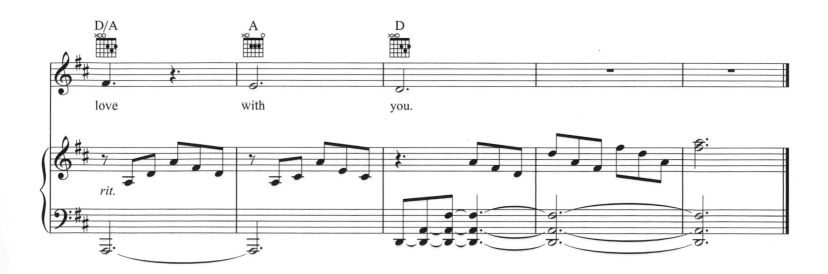

CARELESS WHISPER

Words and Music by GEORGE MICHAEL
and ANDREW RIDGELEY

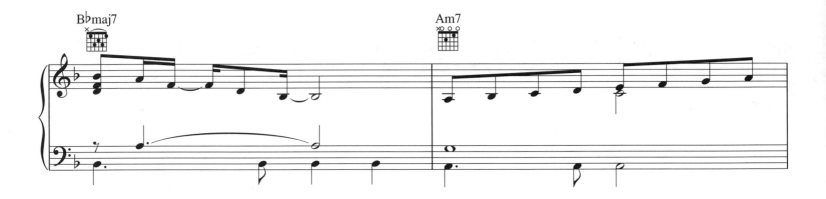

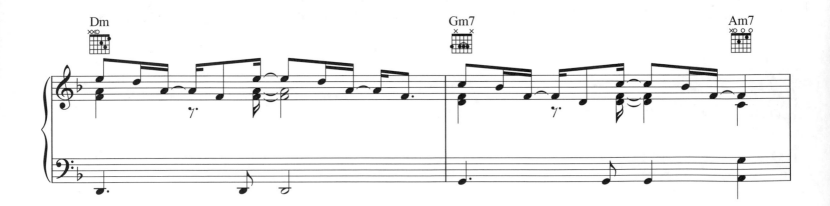

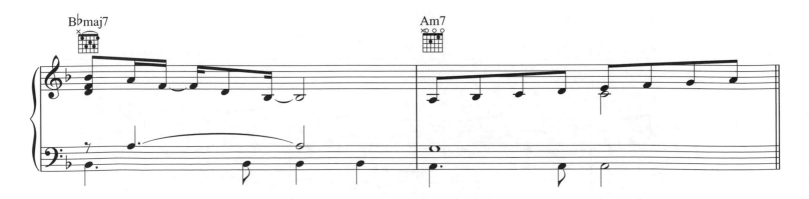

way I dance __ with you, oh. ____

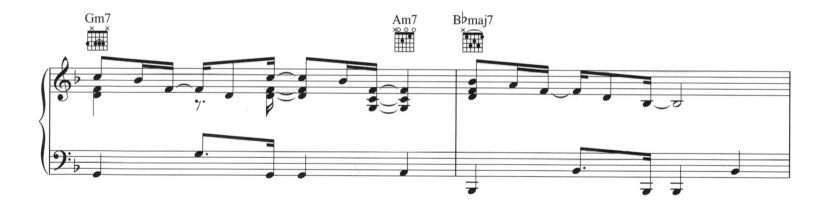

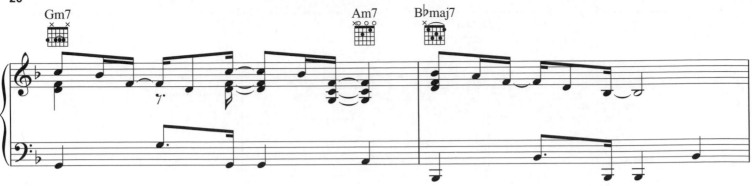

To - night the mu - sic seems so loud, __ I

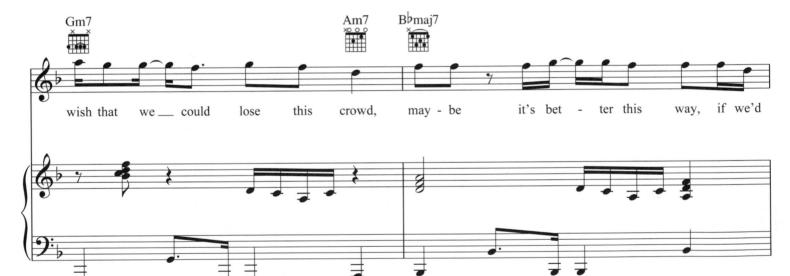

wish that we __ could lose this crowd, may - be it's bet - ter this way, if we'd

hurt each oth - er with the things we want to say. __ We could-'ve been __ so good to-geth - er, we

waste a chance that I've_ been giv-en, so I'm nev-er gon-na dance a-gain_ the

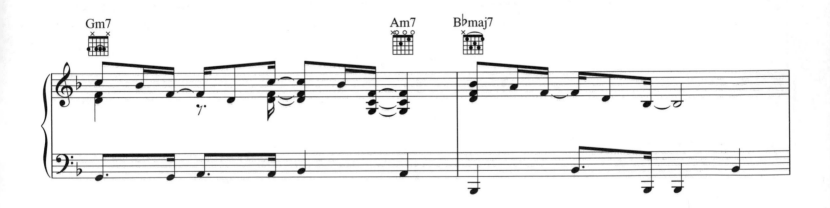

way I dance_ with you. _____

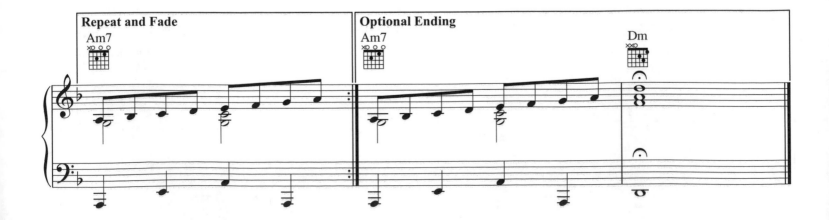

Repeat and Fade

Optional Ending

(Everything I Do)
I DO IT FOR YOU

from the Motion Picture ROBIN HOOD: PRINCE OF THIEVES

Words and Music by BRYAN ADAMS,
R.J. LANGE and MICHAEL KAMEN

you. There's no love like

your love, _____ and no oth - er could give

more _____ love. There's no _____ way, _____ un - less

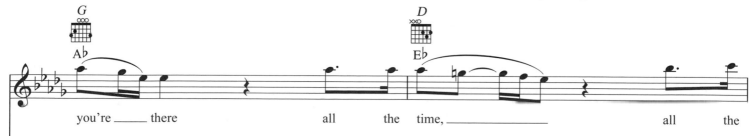

you're _____ there all the time, _____ all the

way, ____ yeah. ____

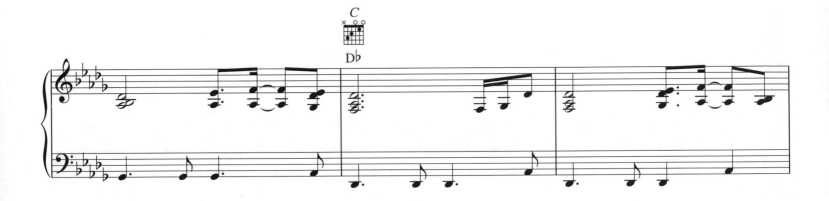

Oh, you can't tell me it's not worth try - ing for. I can't

EBONY AND IVORY

Words and Music by
PAUL McCARTNEY

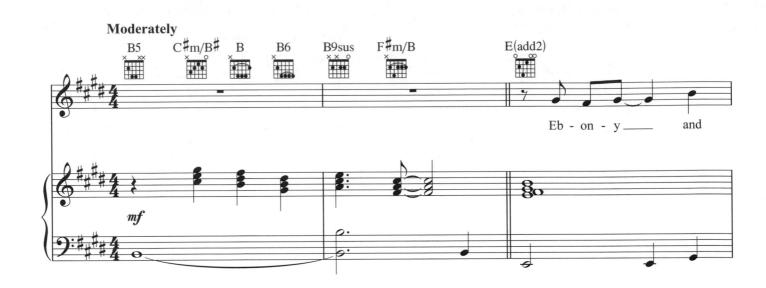

Ebony and

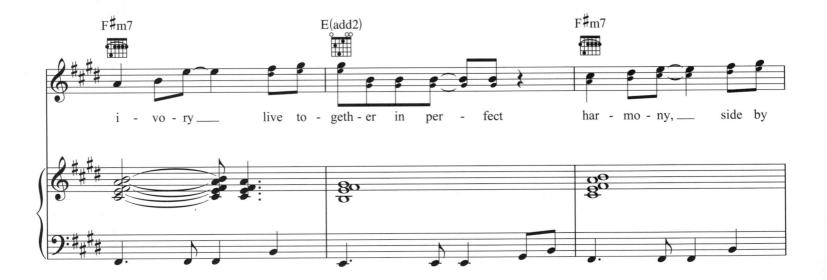

i-vo-ry____ live to-geth-er in per-fect har-mo-ny,____ side by

side on my pian-o key-board, oh____ Lord, why____ don't we?____

to sur - vive, ___ to - geth - er a - live. ___

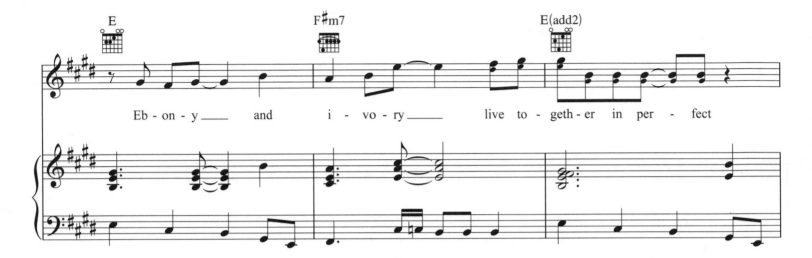

Eb - on - y ___ and i - vo - ry ___ live to - geth - er in per - fect

har - mo - ny, ___ side by side on my pian - o key - board, oh ___ Lord, why ___

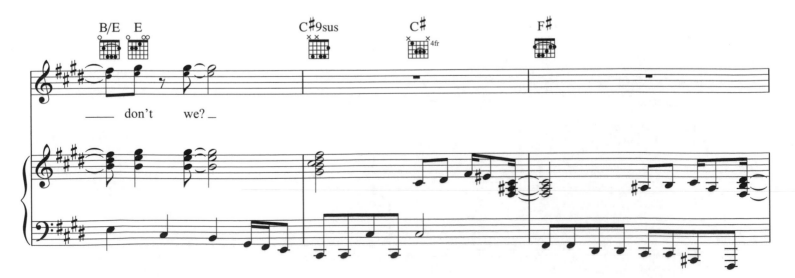

___ don't we? ___

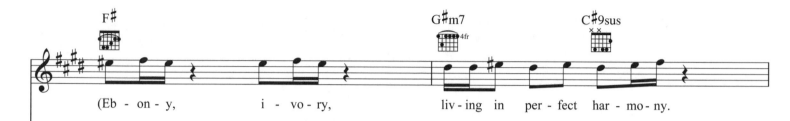

(Eb - on - y, i - vo - ry, liv - ing in per - fect har - mo - ny.

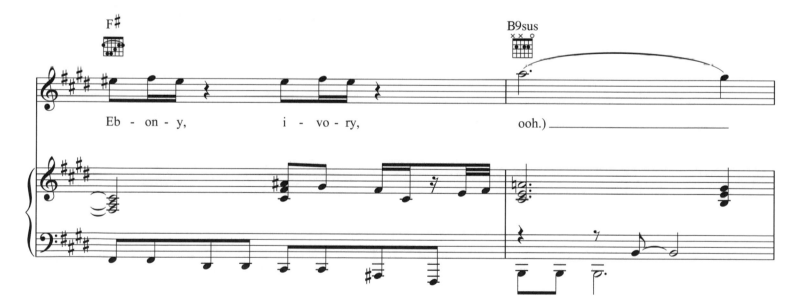

Eb - on - y, i - vo - ry, ooh.)

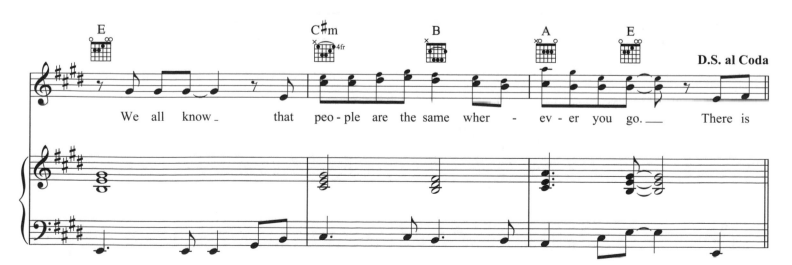

We all know _ that peo - ple are the same wher - ev - er you go. _ There is

don't we? Side by side on my pian - o key -

- board, oh Lord, why don't we?

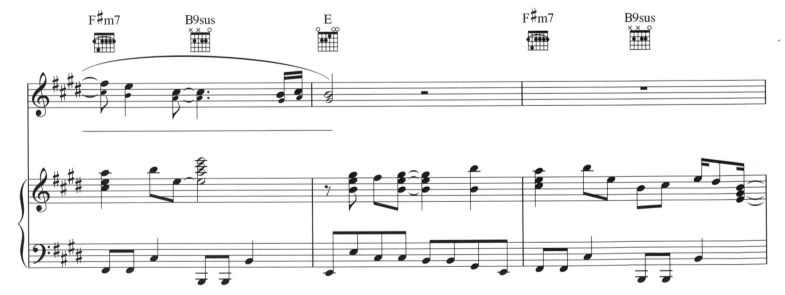

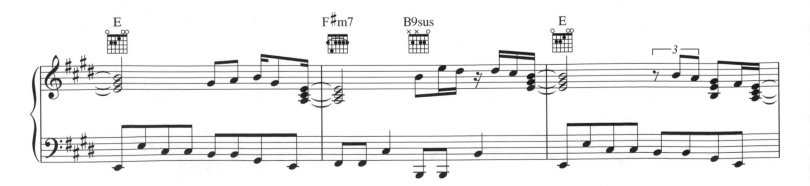

FAITHFULLY

Words and Music by
JONATHAN CAIN

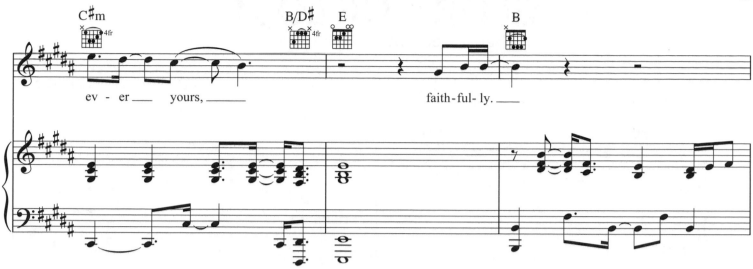

ev - er yours, _____ faith-ful- ly. _____

1. Whoa, _____

2.–5. *(Guitar and vocal ad lib.)*

Whoa, _____

Whoa. _____

GLORY OF LOVE
Theme from KARATE KID PART II

Words and Music by DAVID FOSTER,
PETER CETERA and DIANE NINI

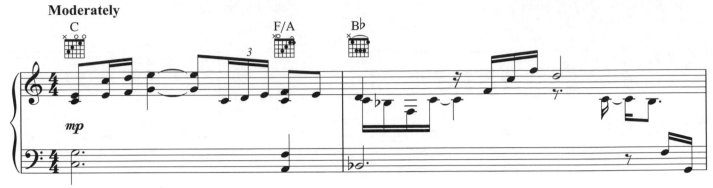

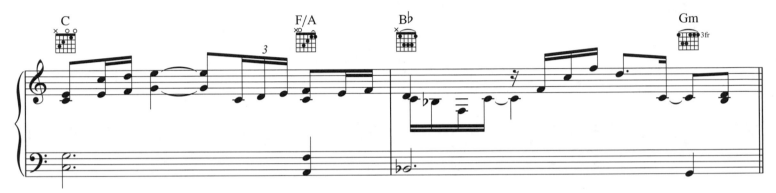

To-night _ it's ver-y clear, as we're both stand-ing here, _

there's _ so man-y things I want _____ to say. _

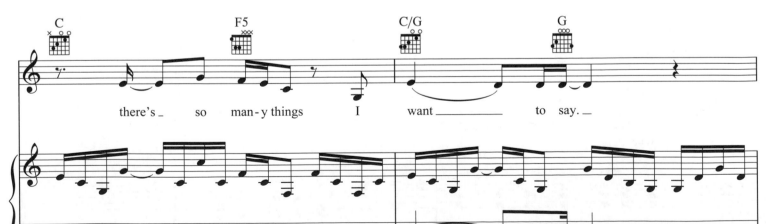

50

I am the man who will fight for your hon - or,

I'll be the he - ro that you're ___ dream - ing of. ___ We're

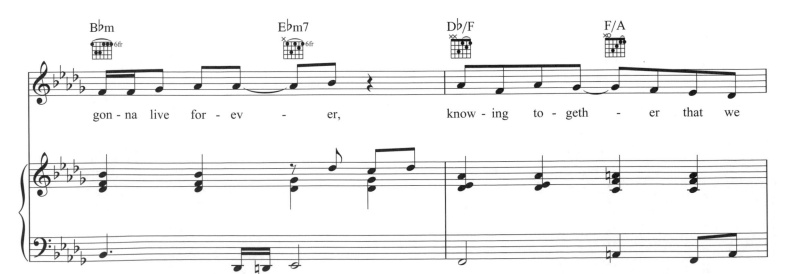

gon - na live for - ev - er, know - ing to - geth - er that we

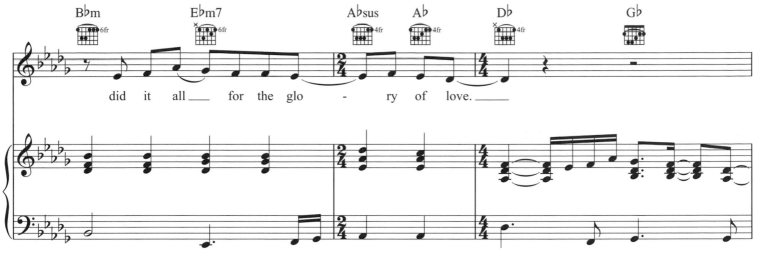

did it all ___ for the glo - ry of love. ___

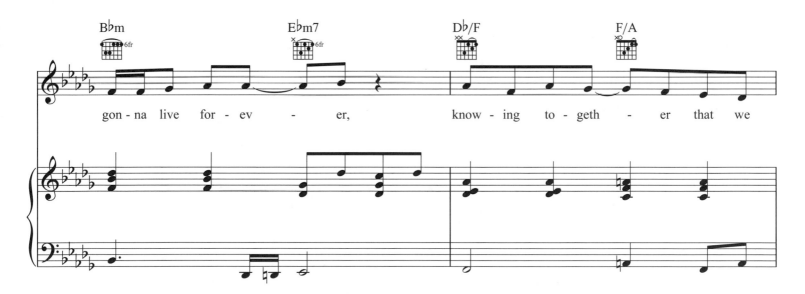

gon - na live for - ev - - er, know - ing to - geth - - er that we

did it all ___ for the glo - ry of love. ___

HELLO

Words and Music by
LIONEL RICHIE

Moderately slow

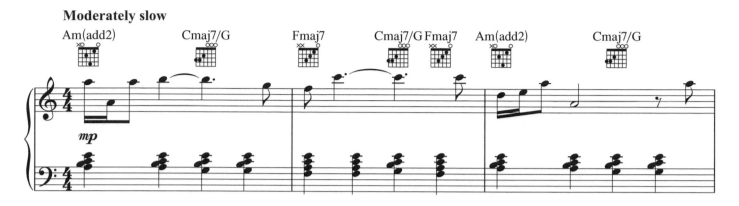

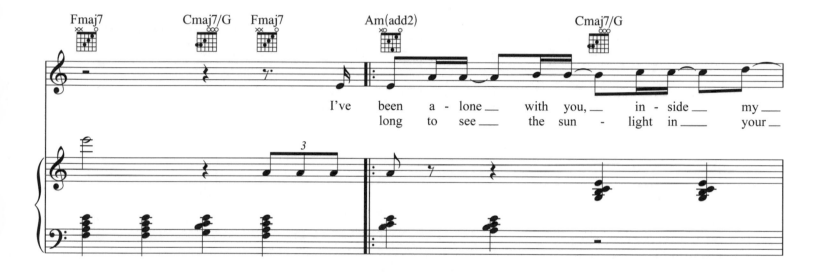

I've been a - lone __ with you, __ in - side __ my __
long to see __ the sun - light in __ your __

__ mind. __
__ hair. __

And in my dreams __ I've kissed your lips
And tell you time __ and time a - gain

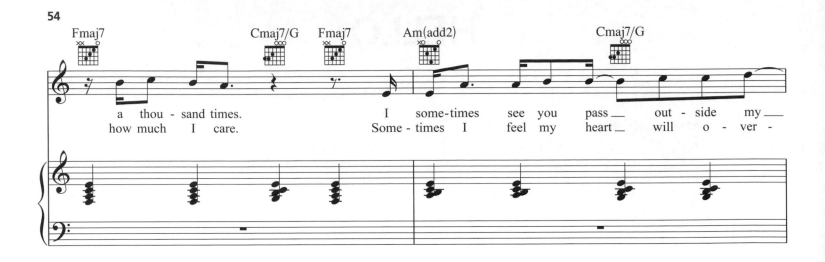

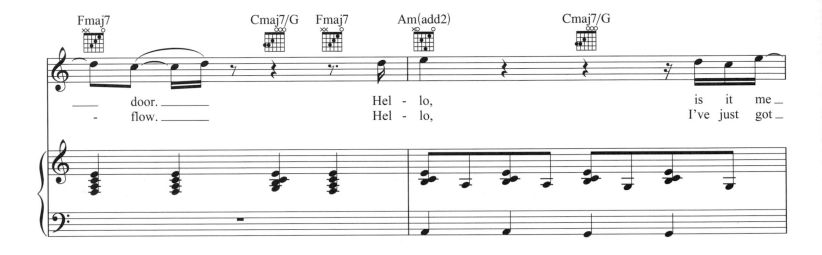

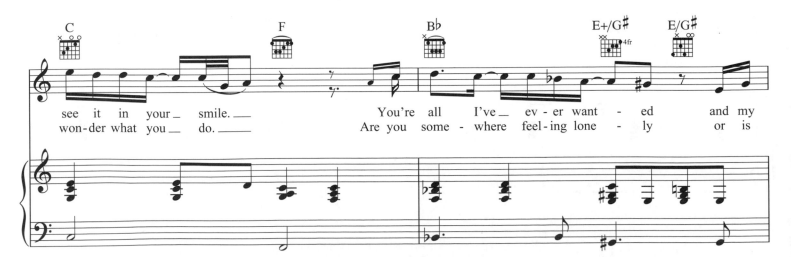

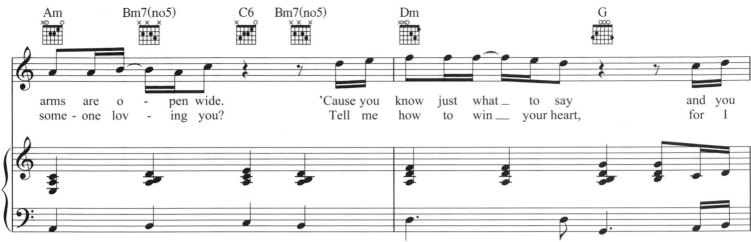

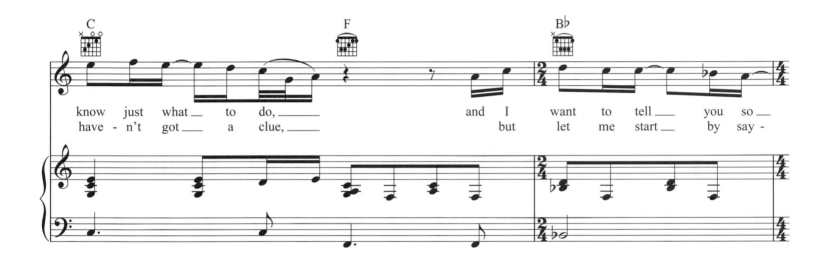

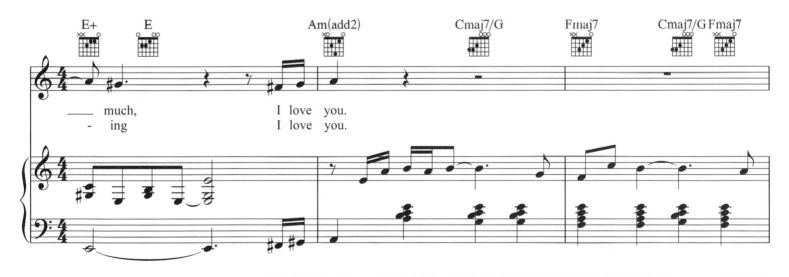

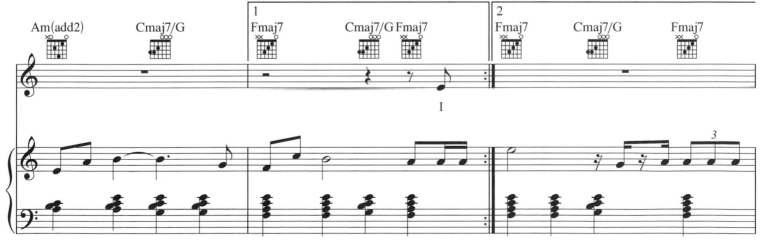

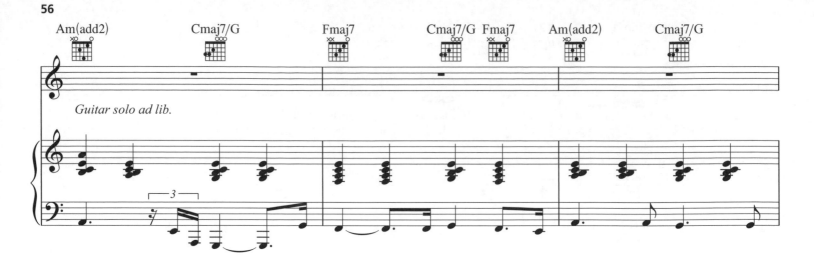

Guitar solo ad lib.

Hel -

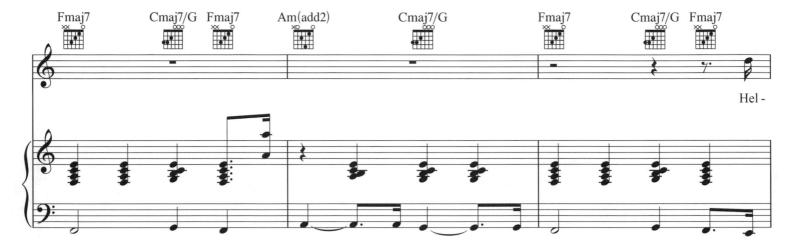

lo,   is it me ___ you're ___ look - ing for? ___   'Cause I

(Solo ends)

won - der where ___ you are, ___   and I won - der what ___ you do. ___   Are you

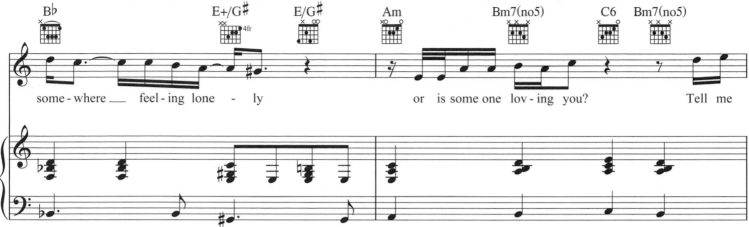

some - where ___ feel - ing lone - ly   or is some one lov - ing you?   Tell me

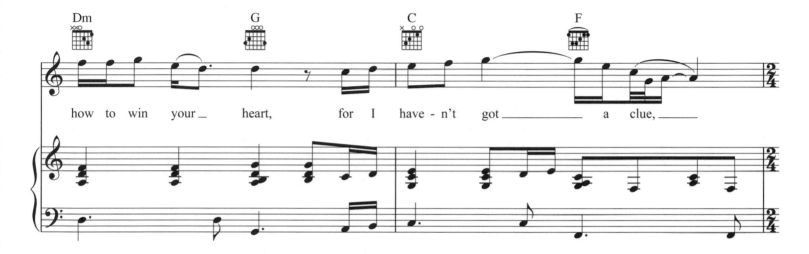

how to win your ___ heart,   for I have - n't got ___ a clue, ___

but let me start by say - ing,   I love

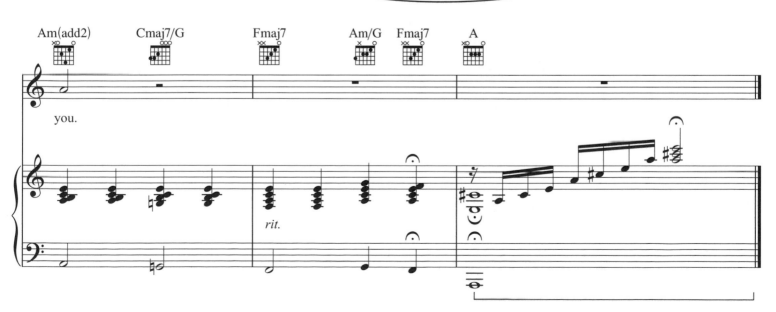

you.

HARD TO SAY I'M SORRY

Words and Music by PETER CETERA
and DAVID FOSTER

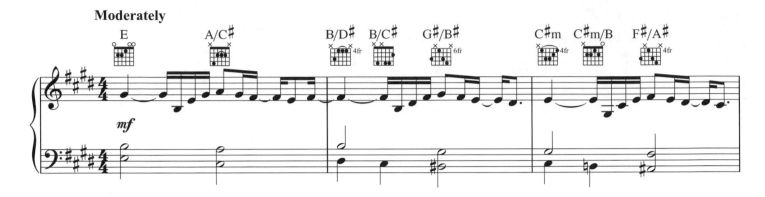

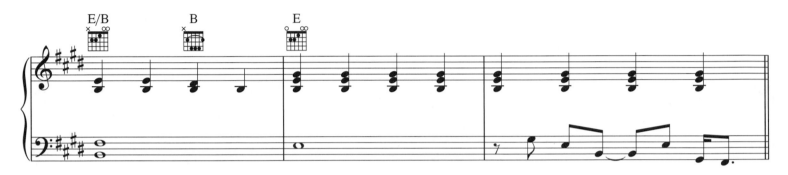

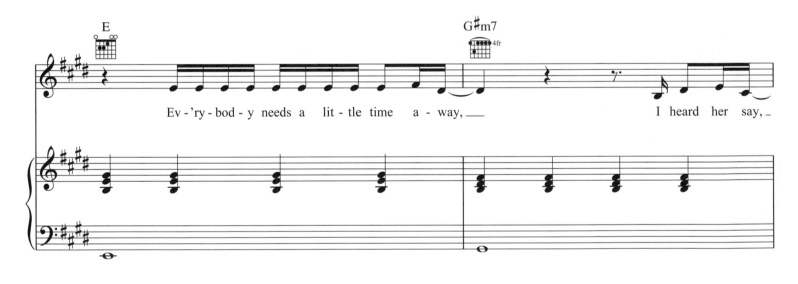

Ev -'ry-bod - y needs a lit - tle time a - way, ___ I heard her say, _

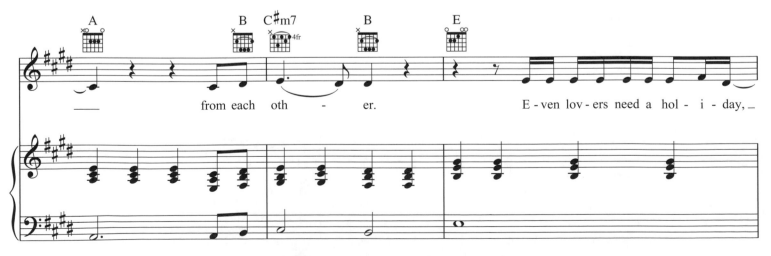

from each oth - er. E - ven lov - ers need a hol - i - day, _

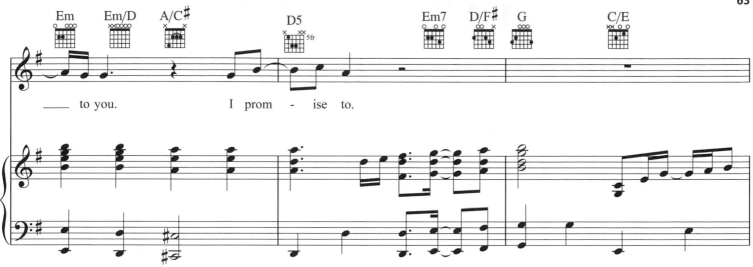

to you. I prom - ise to.

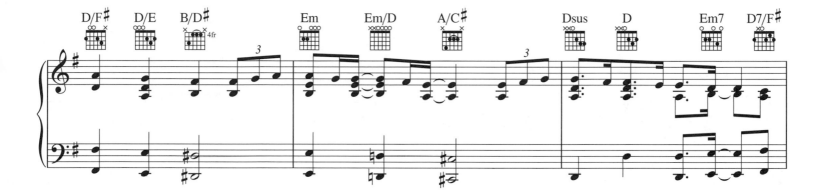

You're gon-na be _ the luck - y one.

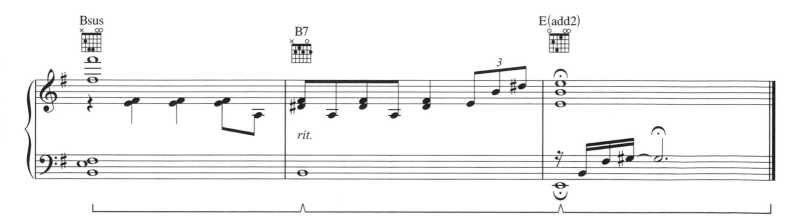

rit.

HERE AND NOW

Words and Music by TERRY STEELE
and DAVID ELLIOT

70

Your love is all __ (I need). __

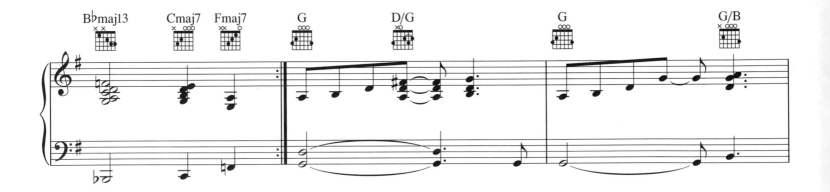

Vocals ad lib. to end

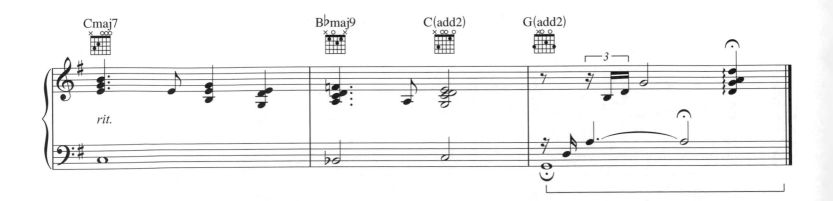

rit.

HERO

Words and Music by ENRIQUE IGLESIAS,
PAUL BARRY and MARK TAYLOR

Moderately

(Spoken:) Let me be your hero.

Would you dance _____ if I asked you to dance? _____

_____ Would you run _____ and nev-er look _ back? _____ Would you

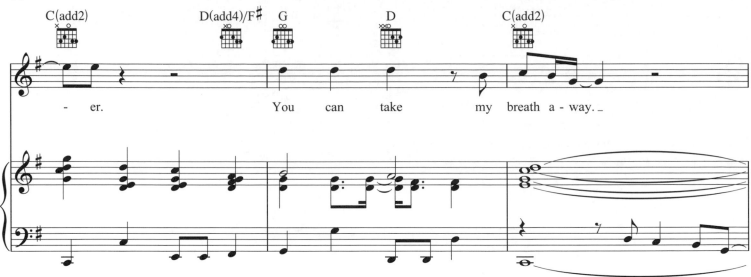

-er. You can take my breath a-way.

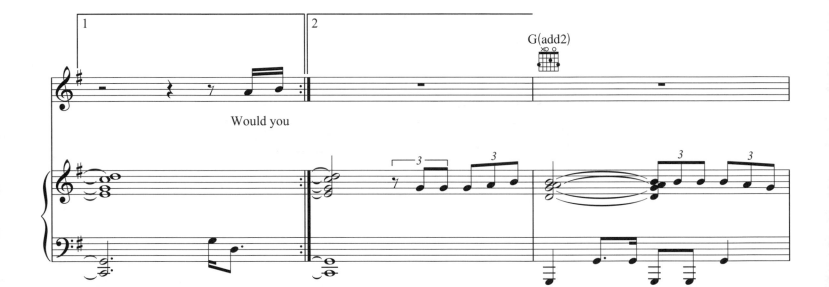

Would you

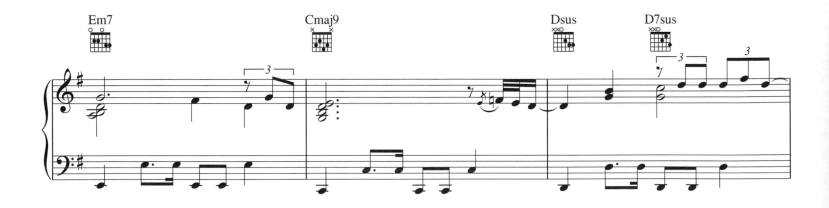

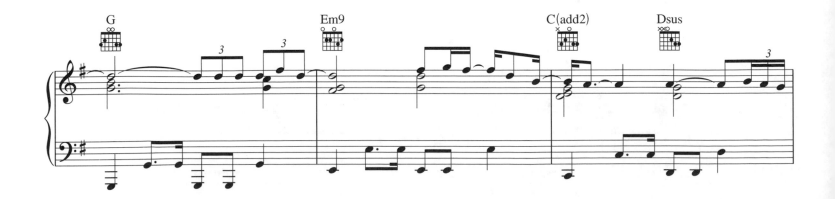

77

HEY JUDE

Words and Music by JOHN LENNON
and PAUL McCARTNEY

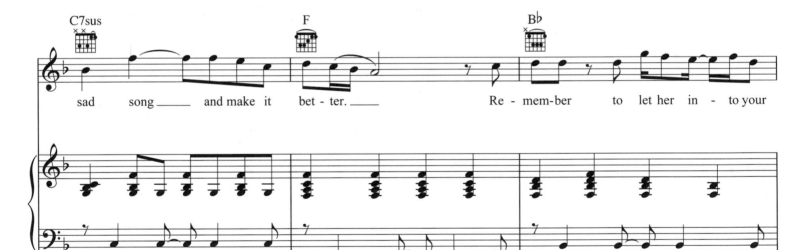

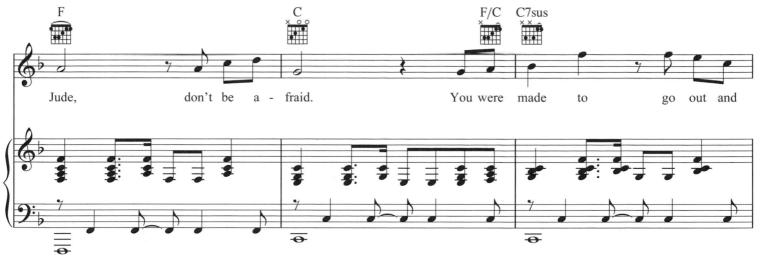

Jude, don't be a - fraid. You were made to go out and

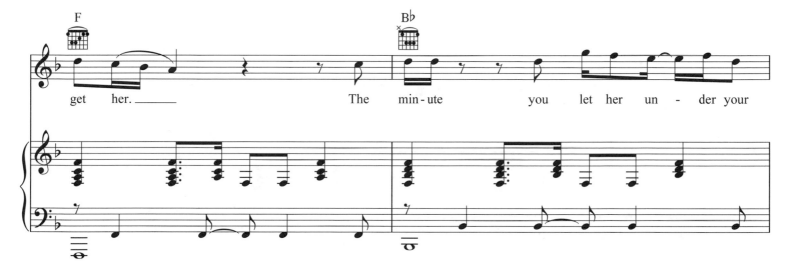

get her. _____ The min - ute you let her un - der your

skin, then you be - gin _____ to make it _____ bet - ter.

And an - y time _____ you feel the pain, _____ hey Jude, _____ re - frain; _____

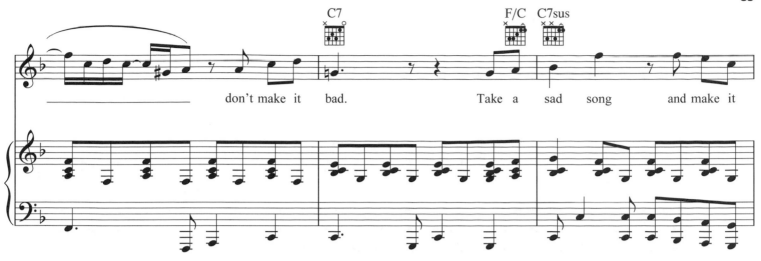

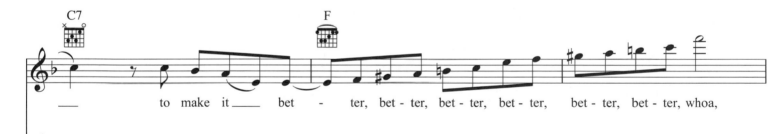

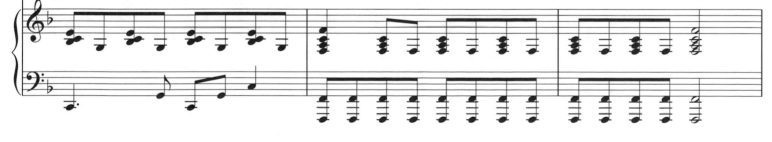

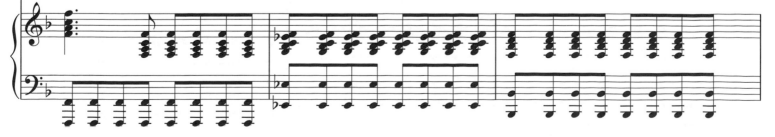

I HONESTLY LOVE YOU

Words and Music by JEFF BARRY
and PETER ALLEN

Moderately slow, expressively

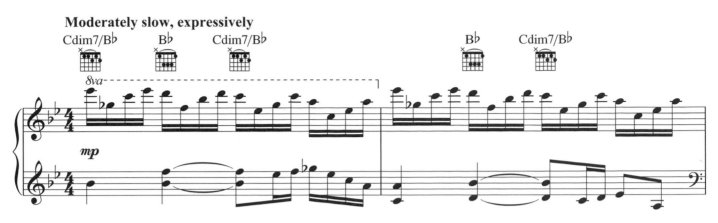

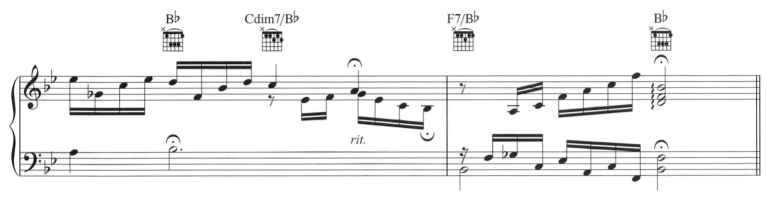

Slightly faster, more steadily

May-be I hang a-round here a lit-tle more than I should; we
You don't have to an-swer; I see it in your eyes.

both know I got some-where else to go. But
May-be it was bet-ter left un-said. But

I love you.

(Spoken:) I love you.

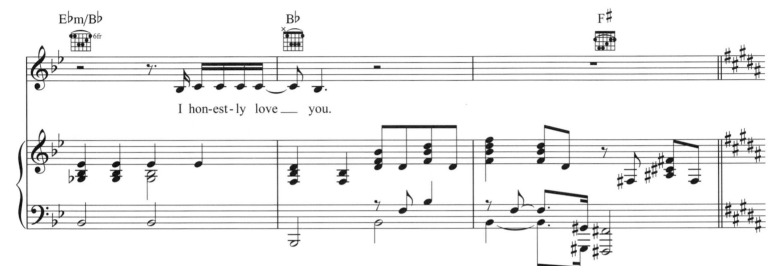

I hon-est-ly love ___ you.

If we both ___ were born _____ in an-oth-er place and time, this

mo-ment might be end-ing in a kiss. But there you are with yours ___ and

here I am __ with mine, __ so I guess we'll just __ be leav - ing it __ at

this. _____ I love you, I hon-est-ly love _

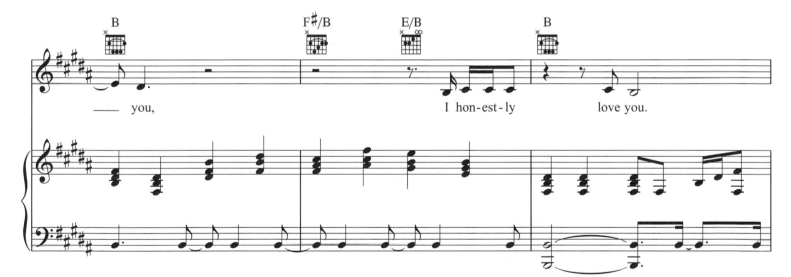

___ you, I hon-est-ly love you.

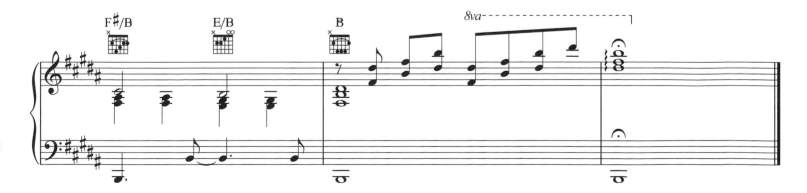

HOW AM I SUPPOSED TO LIVE WITHOUT YOU

Words and Music by MICHAEL BOLTON
and DOUG JAMES

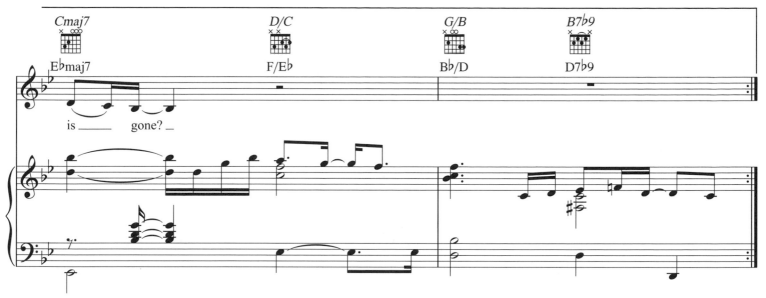

is _____ gone? _

all that I've ____ been liv - ing for _ is _____ gone? _

Guitar solo ad lib.

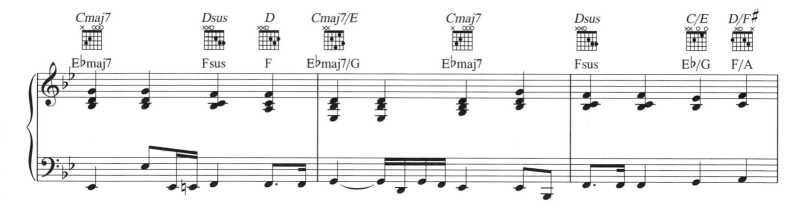

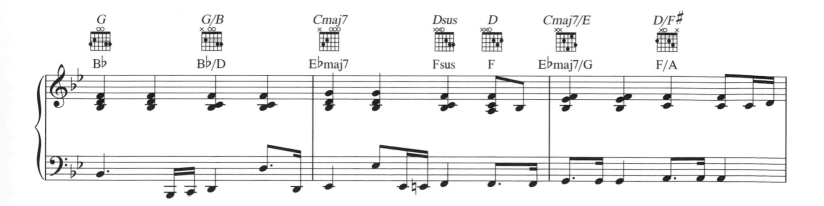

I JUST CAN'T STOP LOVING YOU

Words and Music by
MICHAEL JACKSON

CODA

I just can't stop lov-ing you. ___ We can

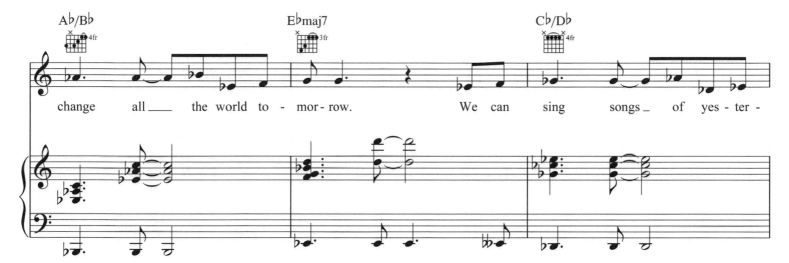

change all ___ the world to - mor - row. We can sing songs ___ of yes - ter -

day. I can say, hey, ___ fare-well to sor - row. This is my

life, and I want to see you for al - ways.

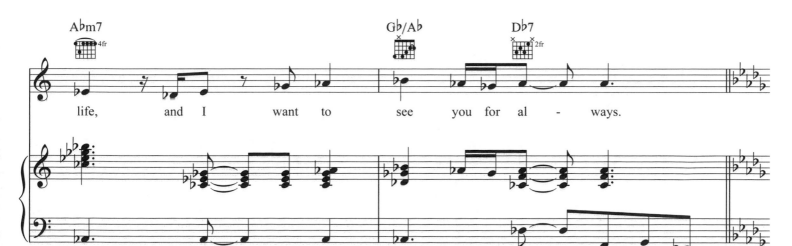

I KNEW I LOVED YOU

Words and Music by DANIEL JONES
and DARREN HAYES

Moderately slow

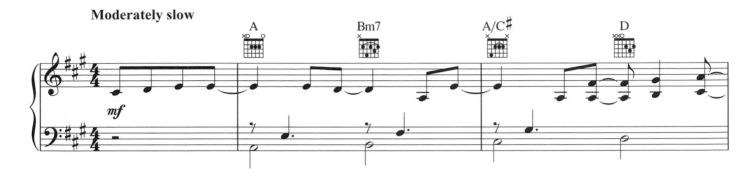

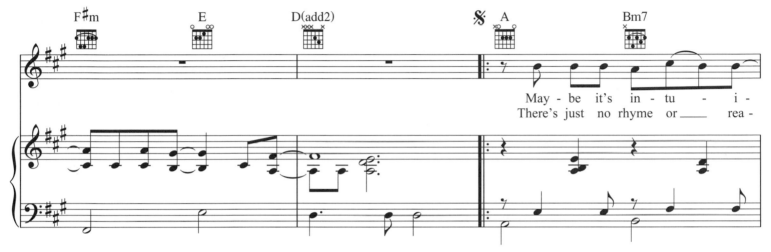

May - be it's in - tu - i -
There's just no rhyme or ___ rea -

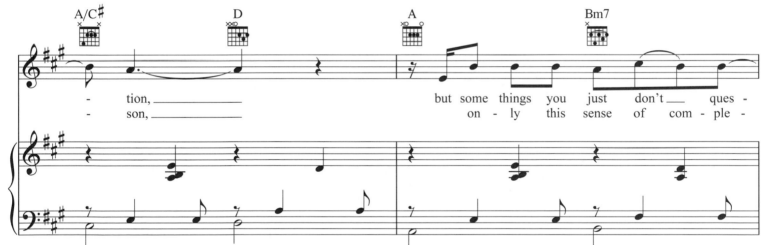

- tion, ___
- son, ___

but some things you just don't ___ ques -
on - ly this sense of com - ple -

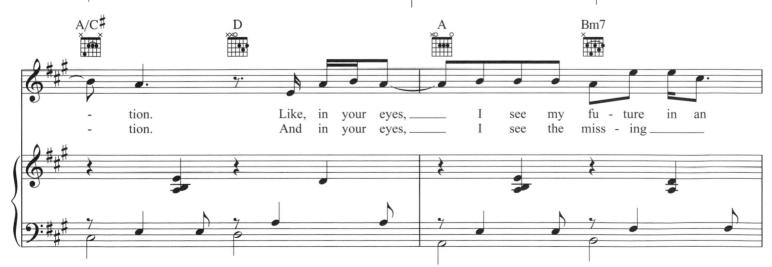

- tion.
- tion.

Like, in your eyes, ___ I see my fu - ture in an
And in your eyes, ___ I see the miss - ing ___

in - stant.___ And there it goes. I think I've found my best ____ friend. __
piec - es ____ I'm search-ing for. I think I've found my way ____ home. __ } I know _

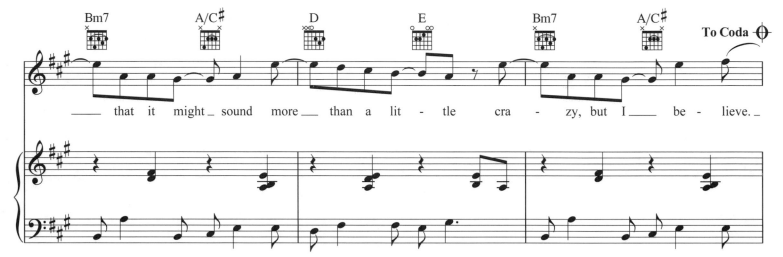

____ that it might __ sound more __ than a lit - tle cra - zy, but I ____ be - lieve. __

To Coda ⊕

N.C.

____ I knew I loved __ you be - fore __ I met ____ you. I think I dreamed __

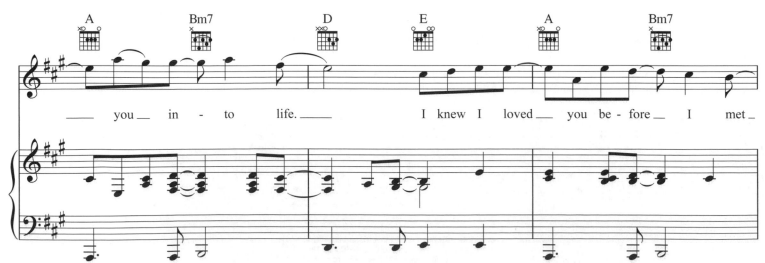

____ you __ in - to life. ____ I knew I loved __ you be - fore __ I met __

D.S. al Coda

you. I have been wait - ing all my life.

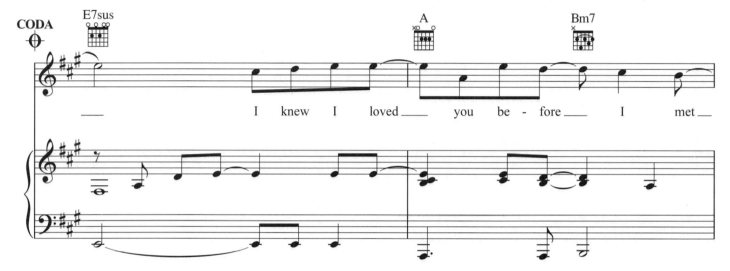

CODA

I knew I loved you be - fore I met

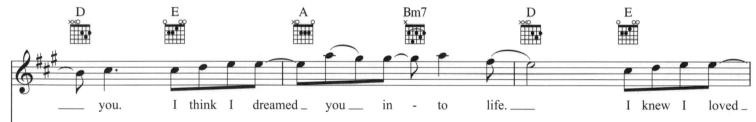

you. I think I dreamed you in - to life. I knew I loved

you be - fore I met you. I have been wait - ing all my life.

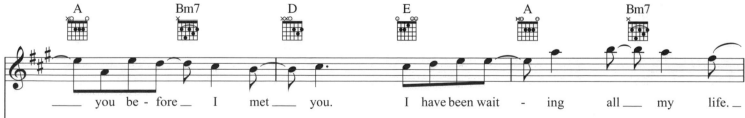

you be - fore ___ I met ___ you. I think I dreamed ___ you ___ in - to life. ___

___ I knew I loved ___ you be - fore ___ I met ___ you. I have been wait -

Repeat and Fade

Optional Ending

- ing all ___ my life. ___ I knew I loved ___ ___

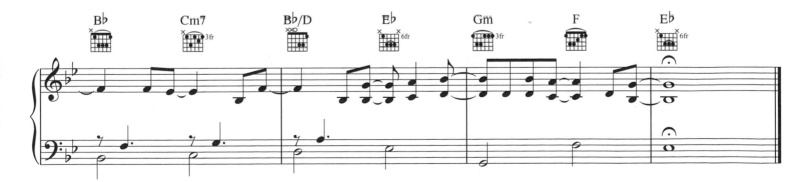

JUST THE WAY YOU ARE

Words and Music by
BILLY JOEL

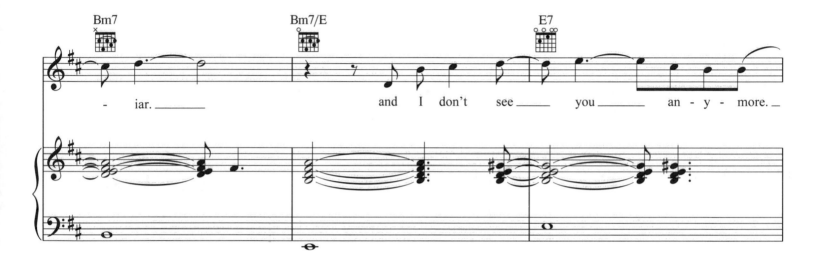

We nev-er could have come _ this _ far. _

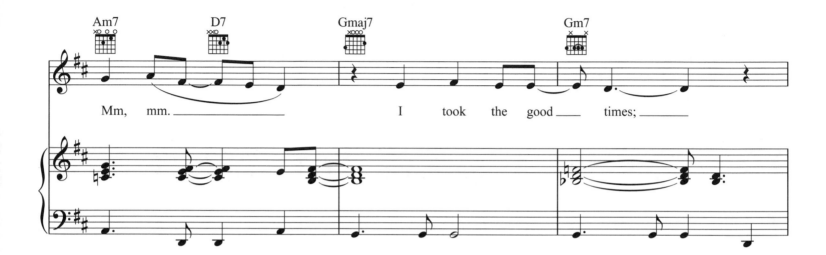

Mm, mm. _ I took the good _ times; _

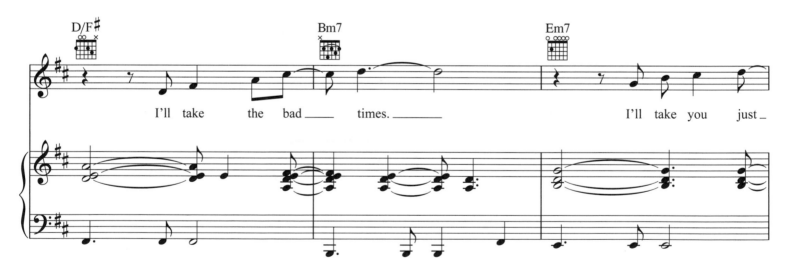

I'll take the bad _ times. _ I'll take you just _

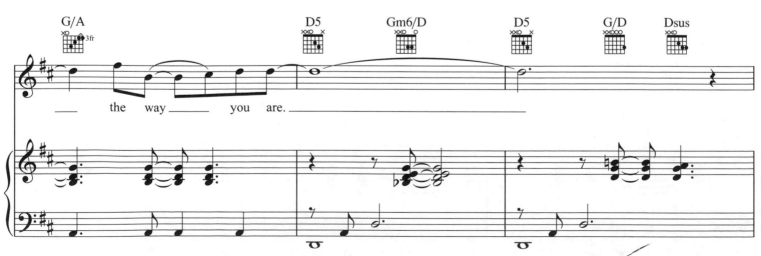

_ the way _ you are. _

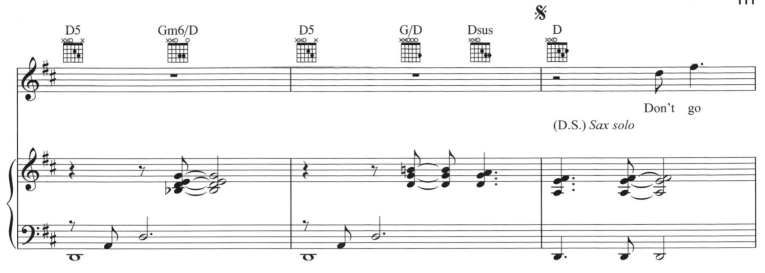

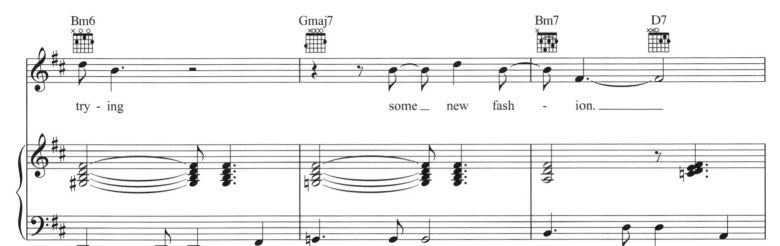

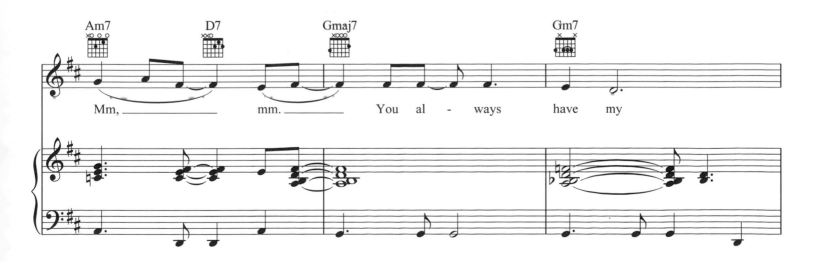

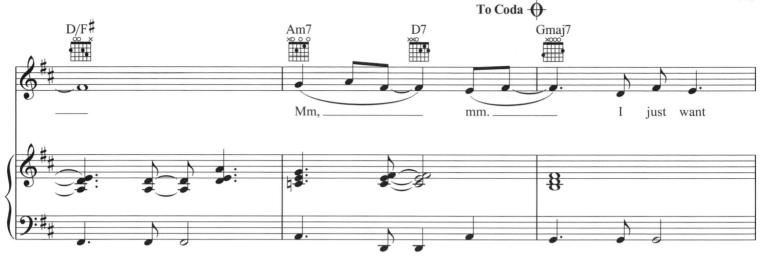

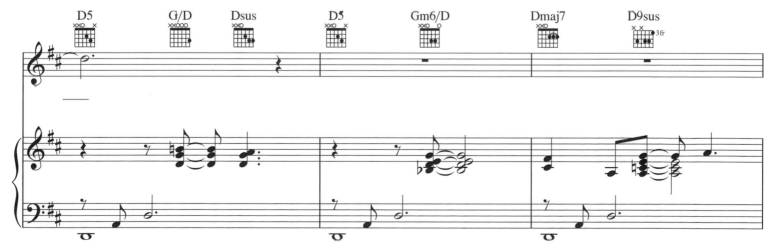

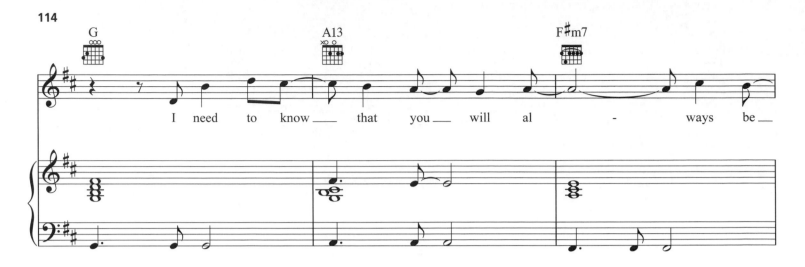

I need to know ___ that you ___ will al - ways be ___

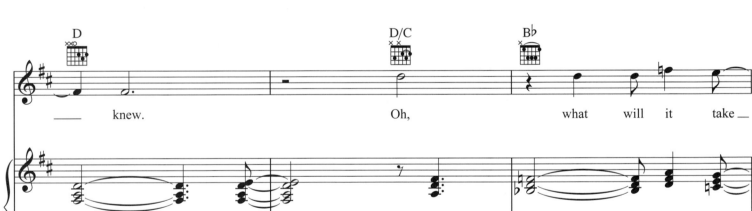

___ the same old some - one that I _____

___ knew. Oh, what will it take ___

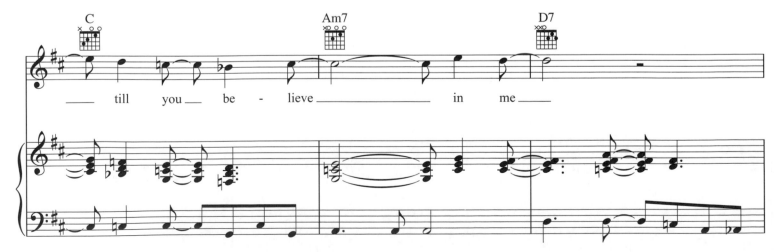

___ till you ___ be - lieve _____ in me _____

the way that I _____ be - lieve _____ in you? _____

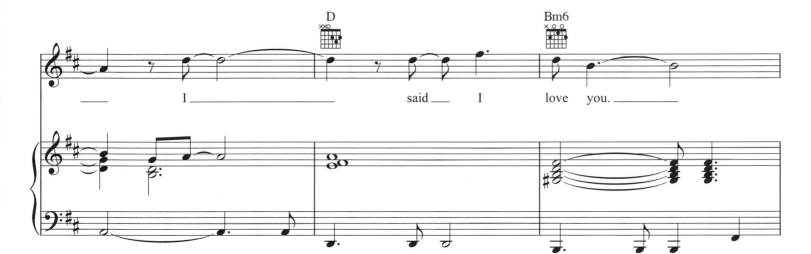

_____ I _____ said _____ I love you. _____

and that's for - ev - er _____ and this I

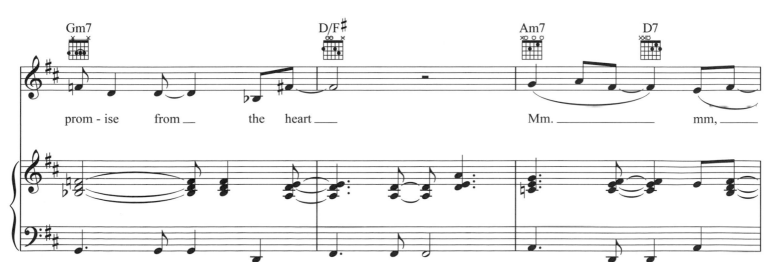

prom - ise from _____ the heart _____ Mm. _____ mm, _____

I could-n't love you an-y bet-

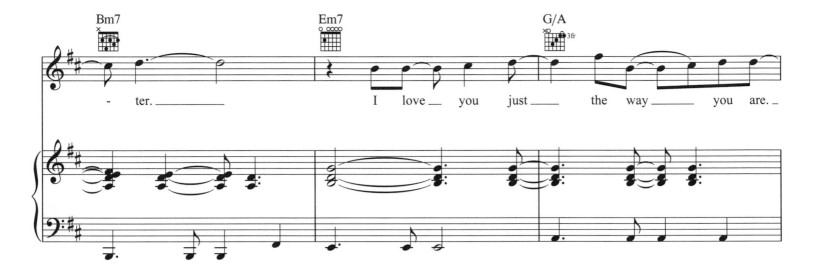

-ter. I love you just the way you are.

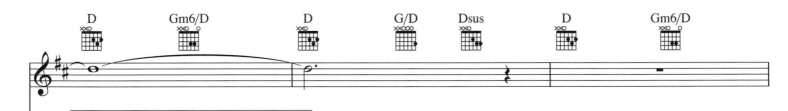

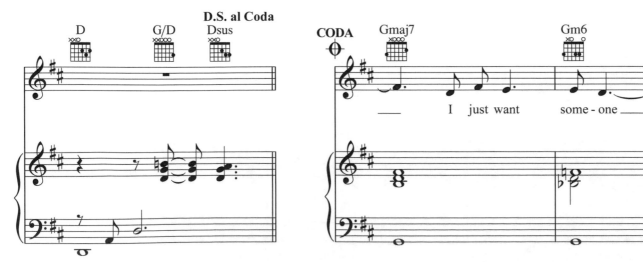

D.S. al Coda

CODA

I just want some-one

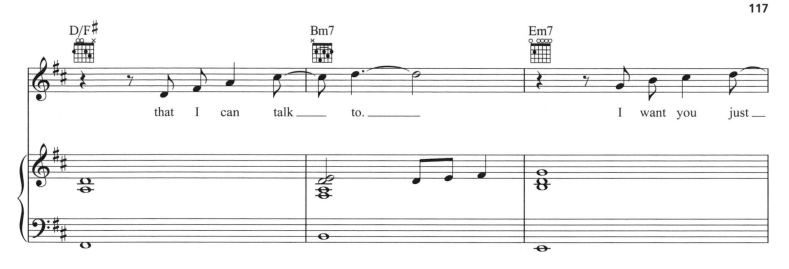

that I can talk to. I want you just

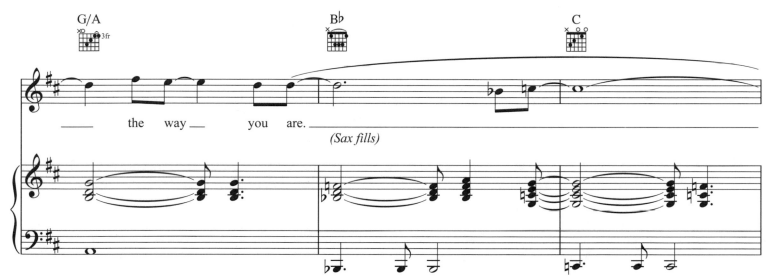

the way you are. *(Sax fills)*

Whoa.

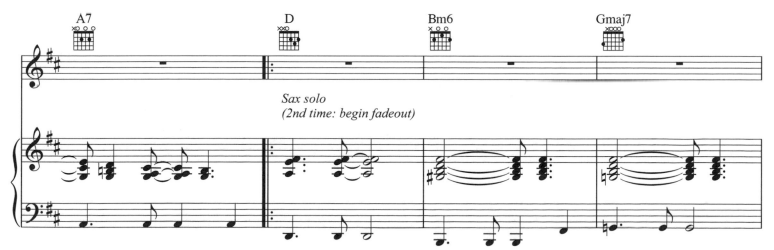

Sax solo
(2nd time: begin fadeout)

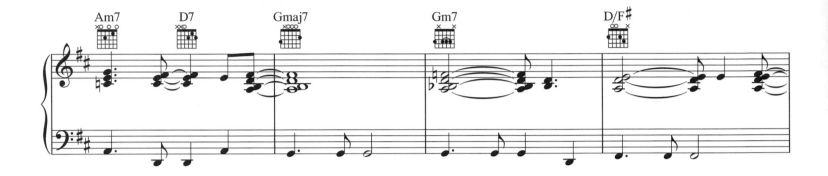

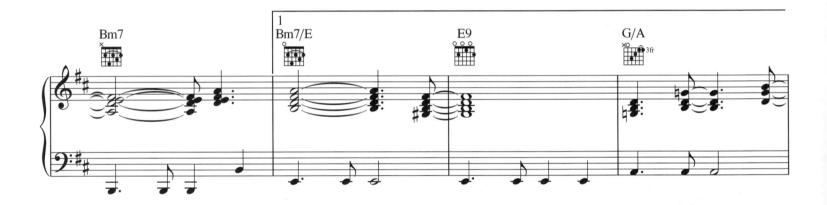

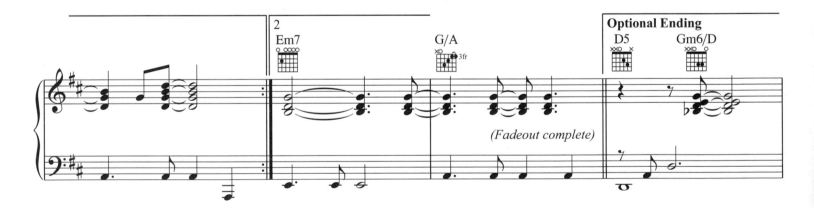

(Fadeout complete)

Optional Ending

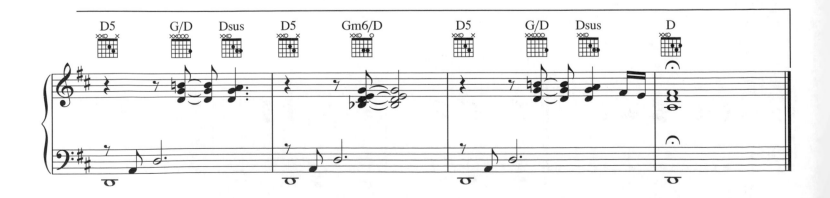

KILLING ME SOFTLY WITH HIS SONG

Words by NORMAN GIMBEL
Music by CHARLES FOX

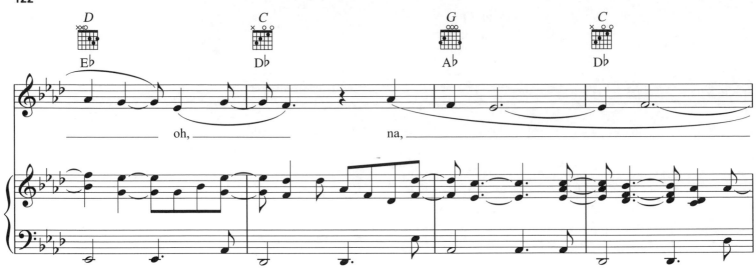

oh, _____ na, _____

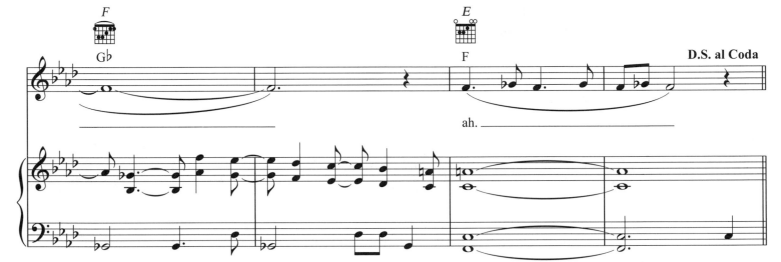

D.S. al Coda

ah. _____

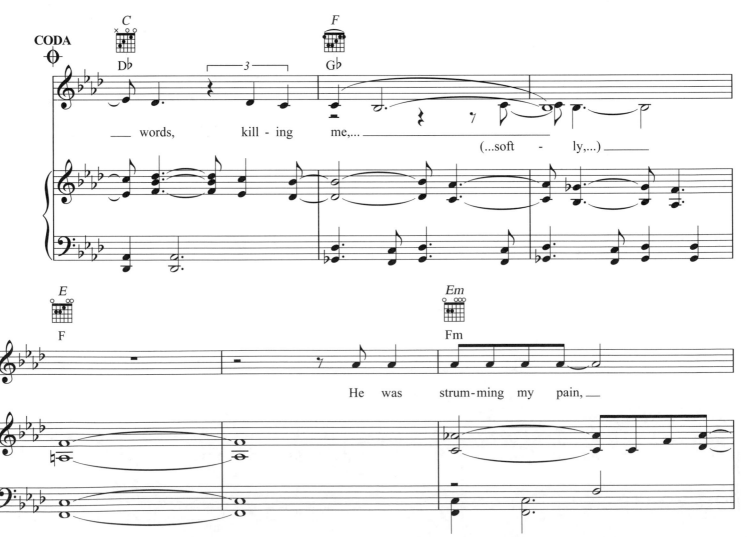

CODA

__ words, kill - ing me,... _____

(...soft - ly,...) _____

He was strum-ming my pain, __

KISS FROM A ROSE

Words and Music by
HENRY OLUSEGUN ADEOLA SAMUEL

Slowly, in 1

eyes be-come large and the light that you shine can't be seen. Ba-

by, _____ I com-pare you to a kiss from a rose _ on the grey. _____ The more I get of you the

strang-er it feels, _ yeah. _____ And now that your rose is in bloom, _ a

light hits the gloom _____ on the _ grey.

light hits the gloom on ___ the ___ grey.

(Ba ya ya ba da ba da da da ba ya ya.

Now that your

Freely

rose is in bloom, a light hits the gloom ___ on ___ the ___ grey. ___

MY HEART WILL GO ON
(Love Theme From 'Titanic')
from the Paramount and Twentieth Century Fox Motion Picture TITANIC

Music by JAMES HORNER
Lyric by WILL JENNINGS

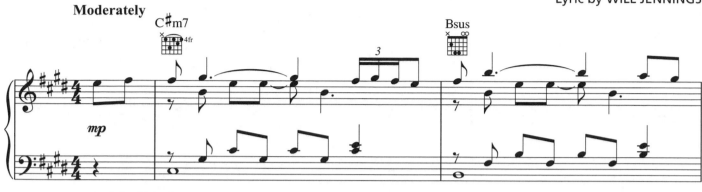

Pedal ad lib. throughout

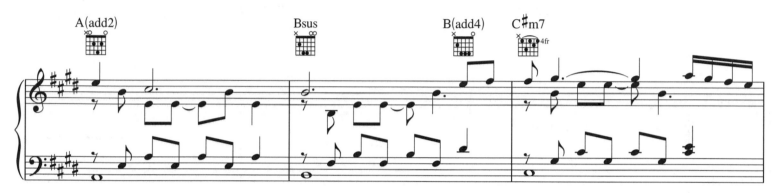

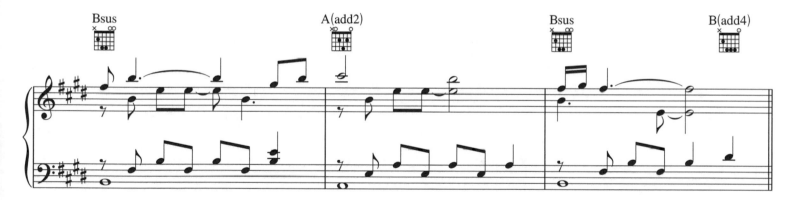

Ev - 'ry night in my dreams I see you, I

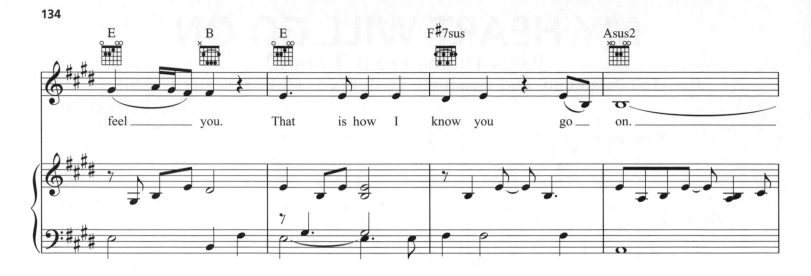

feel _____ you. That is how I know you go __ on. _____

_____ Far a-cross the __ dis - tance and

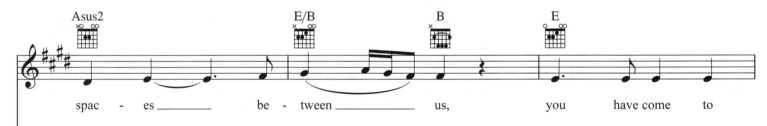

spac - es _____ be - tween _____ us, you have come to

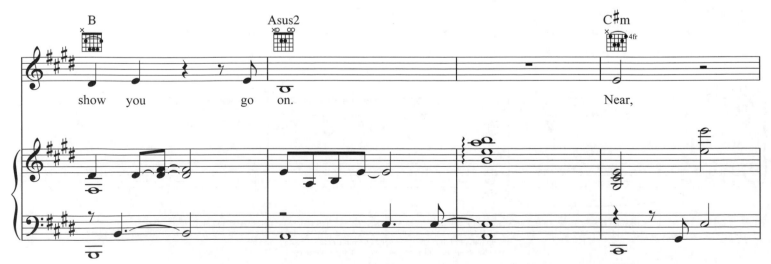

show you go on. Near,

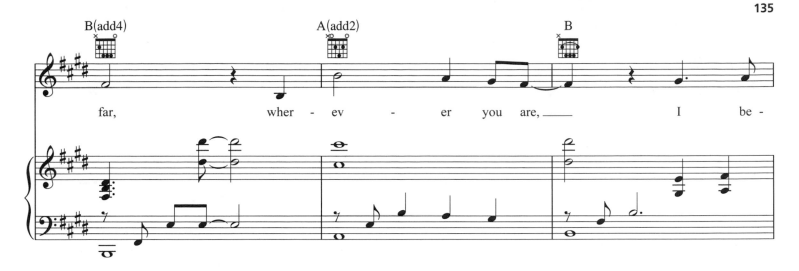

far, wher - ev - er you are, ___ I be -

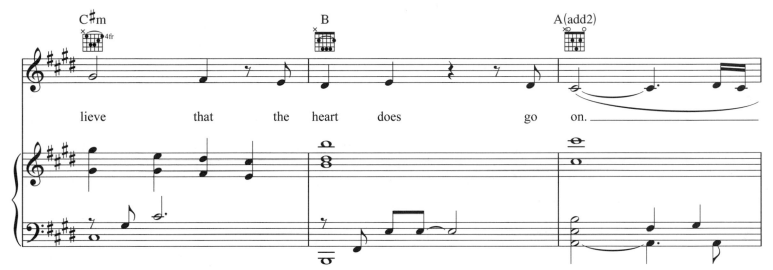

lieve that the heart does go on. ___

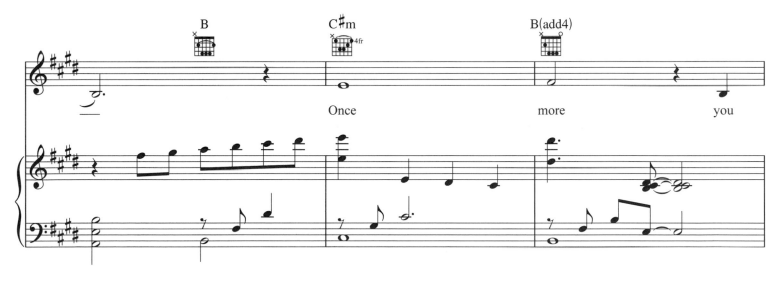

Once more you

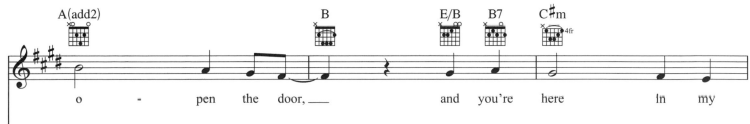

o - pen the door, ___ and you're here In my

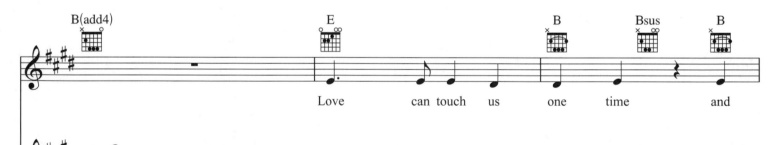

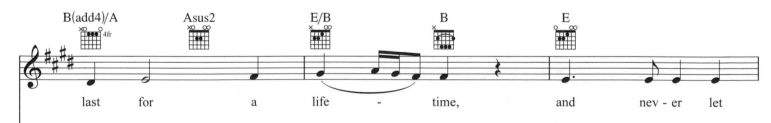

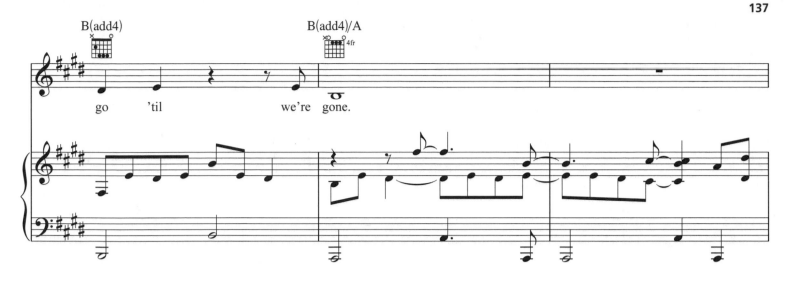

go 'til we're gone.

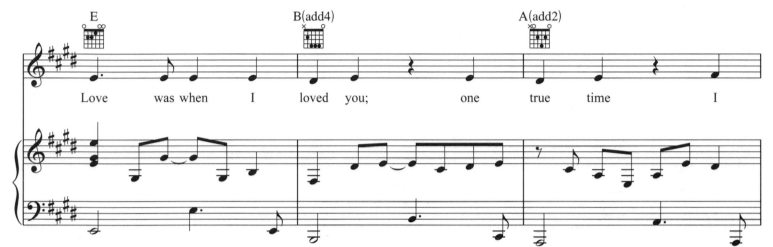

Love was when I loved you; one true time I

hold _____ you; in my life we'll al - ways go __

on. _____ Near,

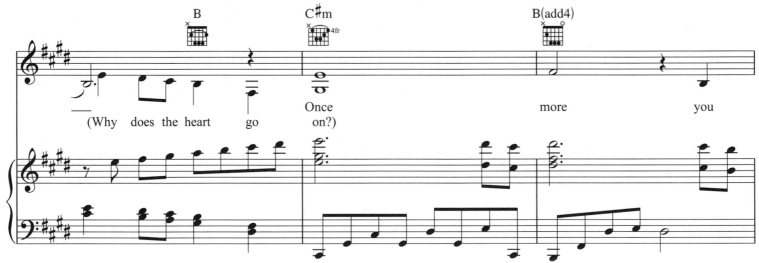

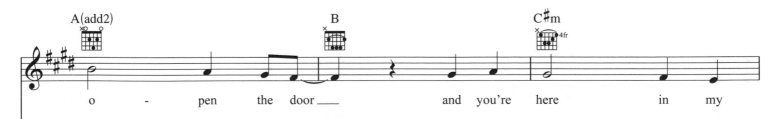

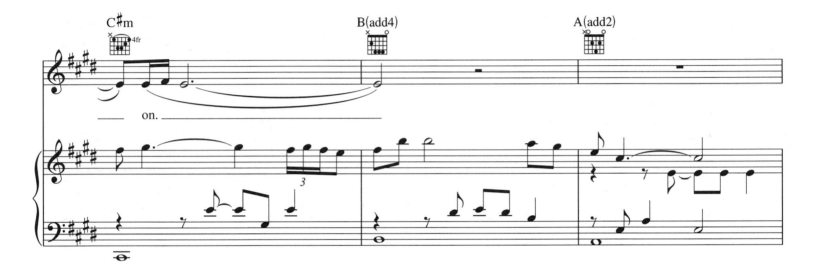

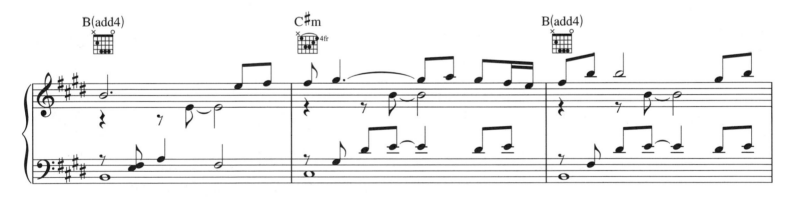

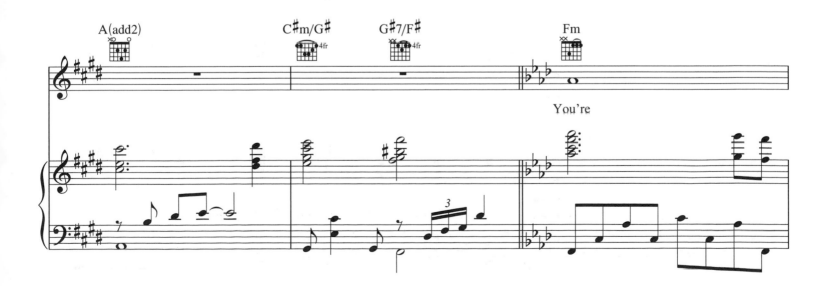

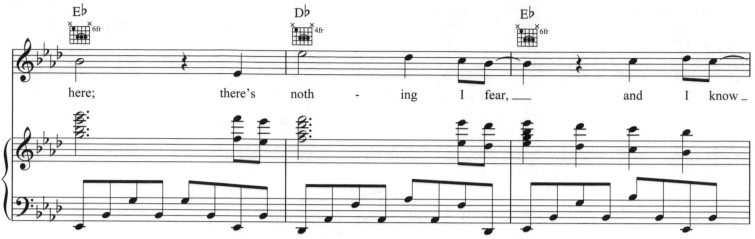

here; there's noth - ing I fear, ___ and I know __

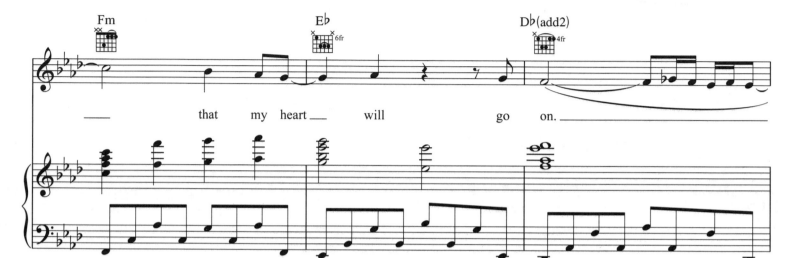

___ that my heart __ will go on. ___

___ We'll stay for -

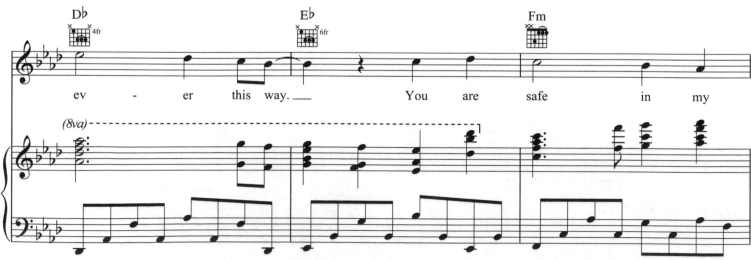

ev - er this way. ___ You are safe in my

RAINY DAYS AND MONDAYS

Lyrics by PAUL WILLIAMS
Music by ROGER NICHOLS

RIGHT HERE WAITING

Words and Music by
RICHARD MARX

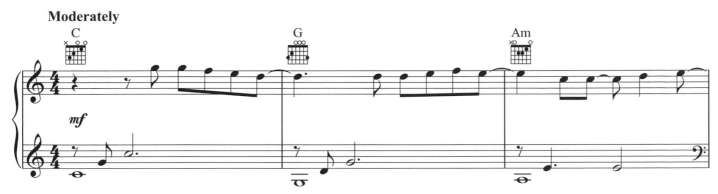

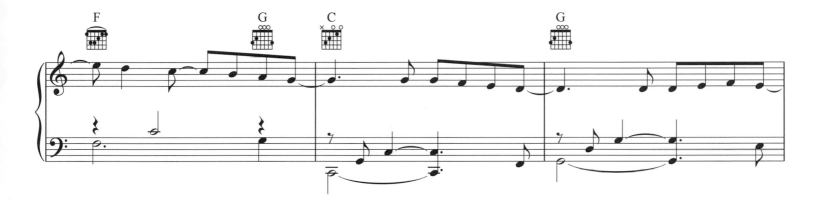

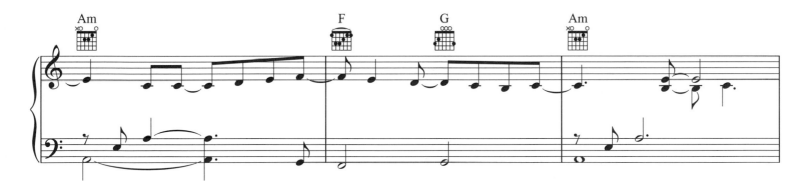

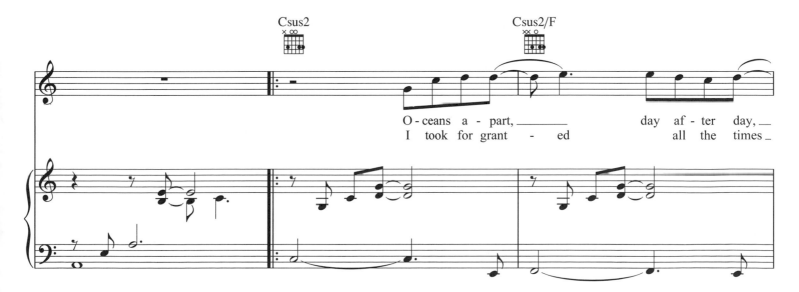

O - ceans a - part, _____ day af - ter day, _____
I took for grant - ed all the times _

this ro - mance. ___

But in the

end, if I'm ___ with you, ___ I'll take ___ the chance. ___

Oh, can't you see ___

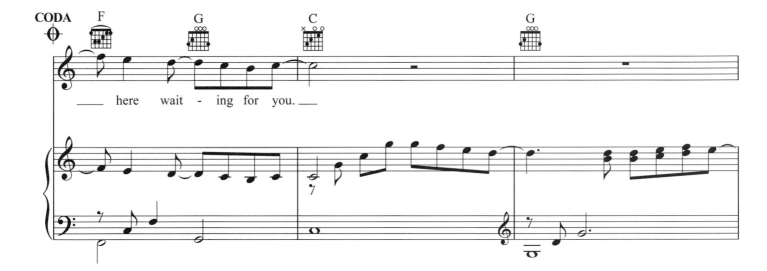

CODA

___ here wait - ing for you. ___

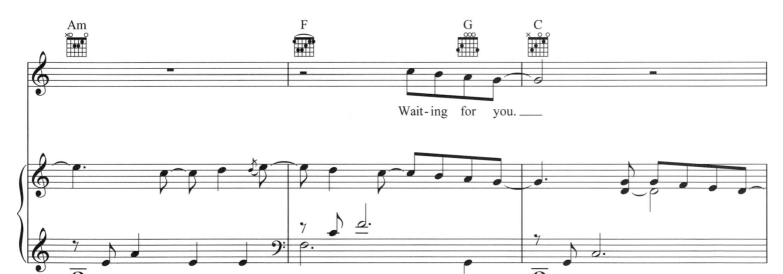

Wait-ing for you. ___

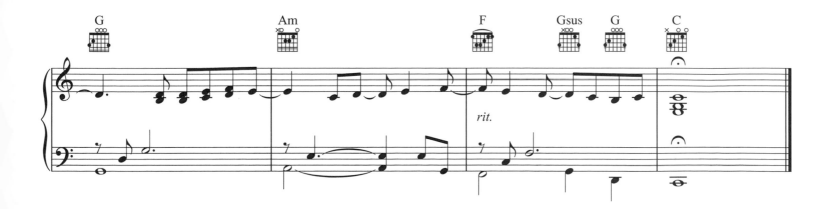

rit.

SAVE THE BEST FOR LAST

Words and Music by WENDY WALDMAN,
PHIL GALDSTON and JON LIND

SHAPE OF MY HEART

Music by STING and DOMINIC MILLER
Lyrics by STING

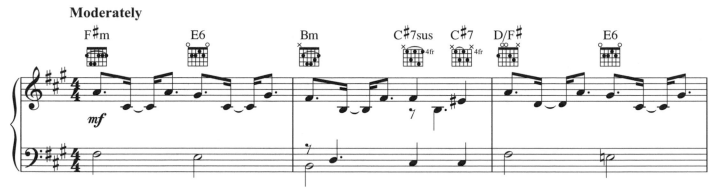

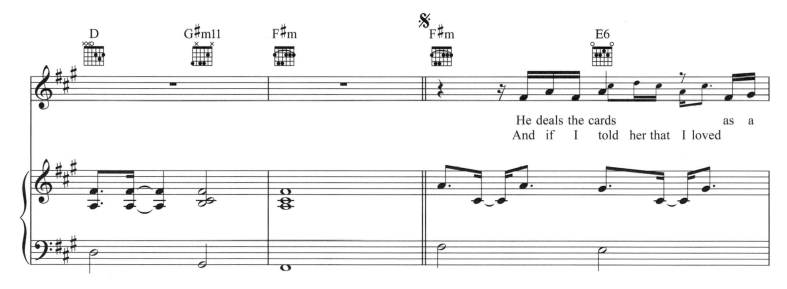

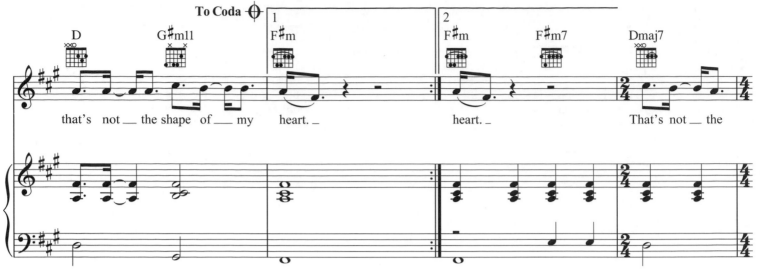

that's not — the shape of — my heart. — heart. — That's not — the

shape, _____ the shape of — my heart. _____

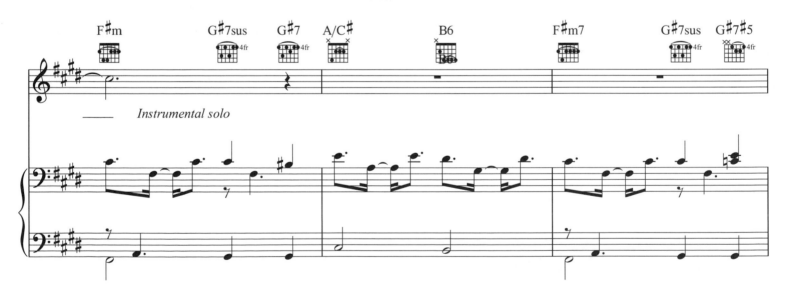

Instrumental solo

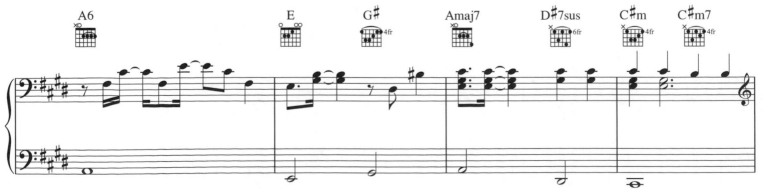

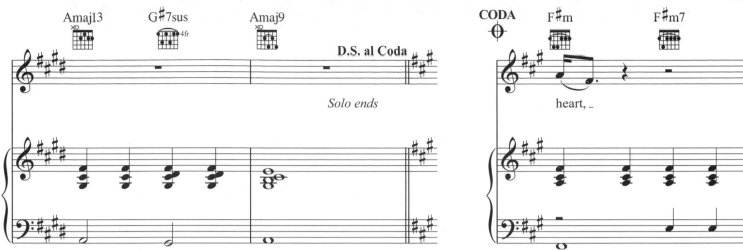

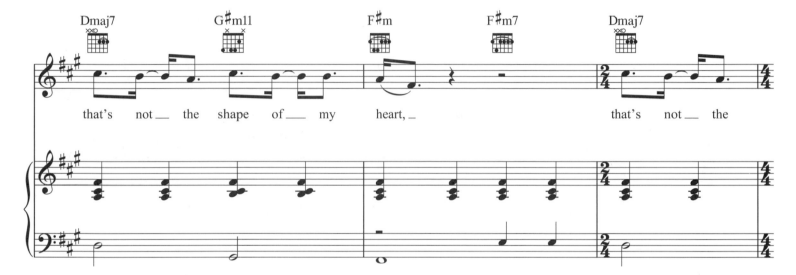

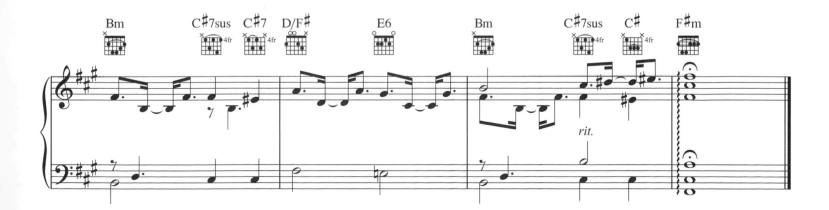

SAVING ALL MY LOVE FOR YOU

Words by GERRY GOFFIN
Music by MICHAEL MASSER

few _____ sto - len mo - ments _____ is all _____ that we share.
not _____ ver - y eas - y liv - ing all a - lone. My

You've _____ got your fam - 'ly _____ and they _____ need you there. Though I
friends _____ try and tell me, find a man _____ of my own. But _____

run a - way to - geth - er; love gives you the right___ to be

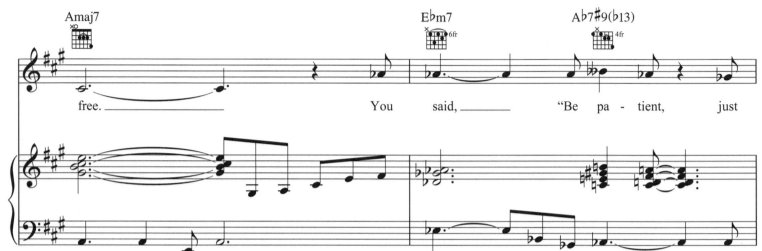

free._____ You said,_____ "Be pa - tient, just

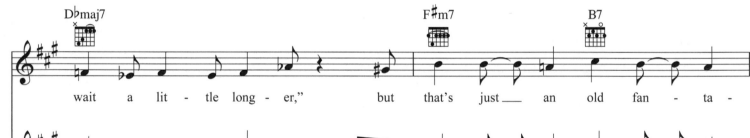

wait a lit - tle long - er," but that's just___ an old fan - ta -

sy._____ I've got___ to get read - y, just a

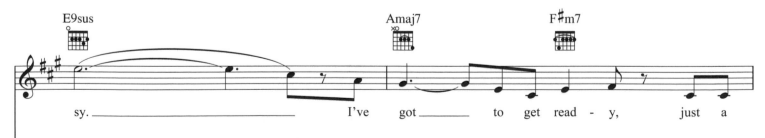

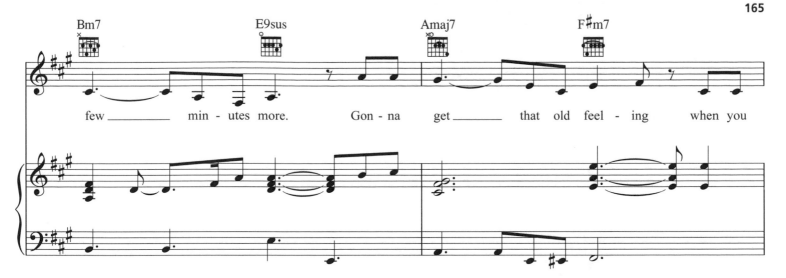

few _____ min - utes more. Gon - na get _____ that old feel - ing when you

walk _____ through that door. 'Cause to - night is the night for ___

feel - ing ___ all ___ right. We'll be mak - ing love the whole night ___

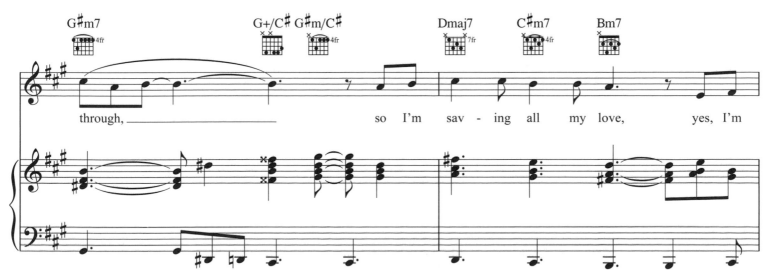

through, _____ so I'm sav - ing all my love, yes, I'm

through, _____ so I'm sav - ing all my love, yeah, I'm

sav - ing all my lov - ing, yes, I'm sav - ing all my love for

Repeat and Fade

you. _____ For

Optional Ending

you. _____

poco rit.

SO FAR AWAY

Words and Music by
CAROLE KING

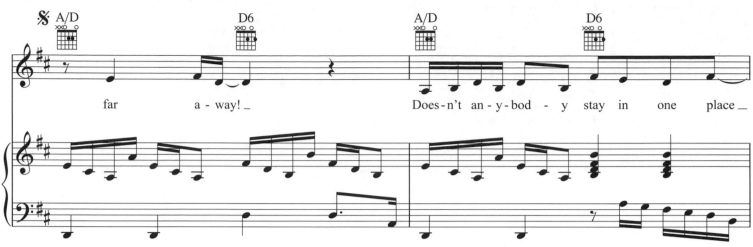

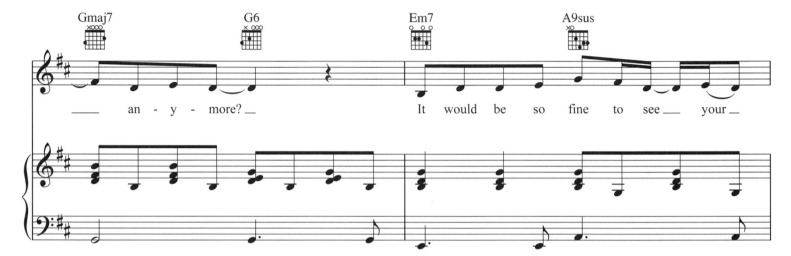

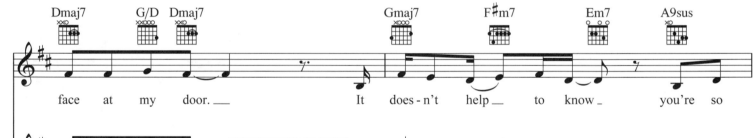

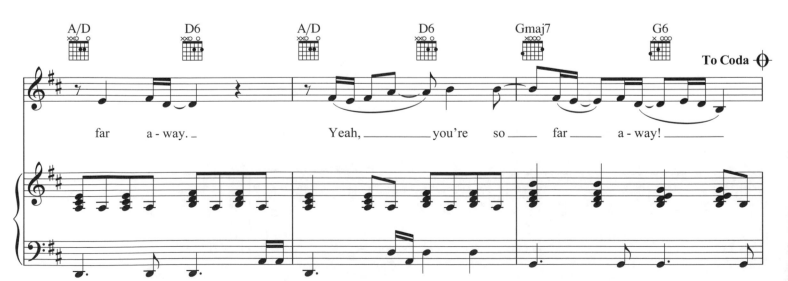

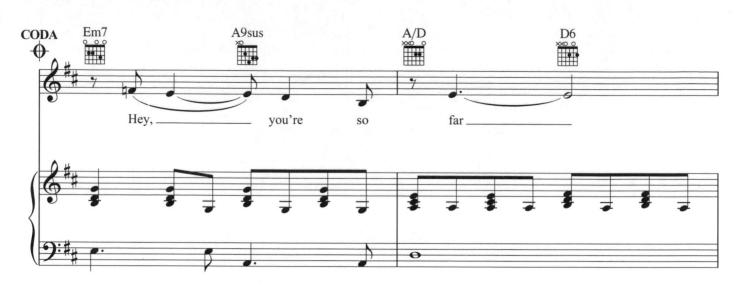

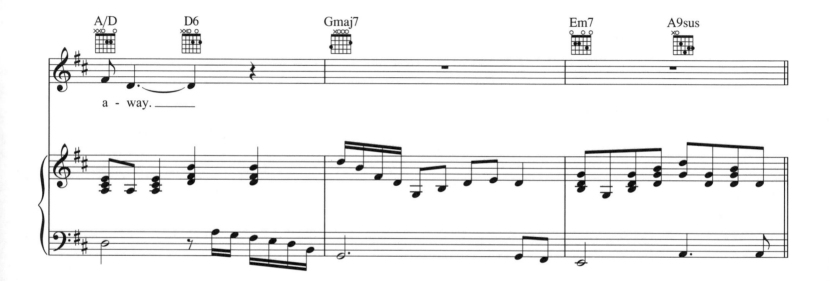

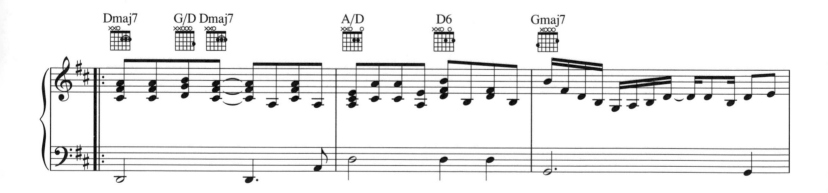

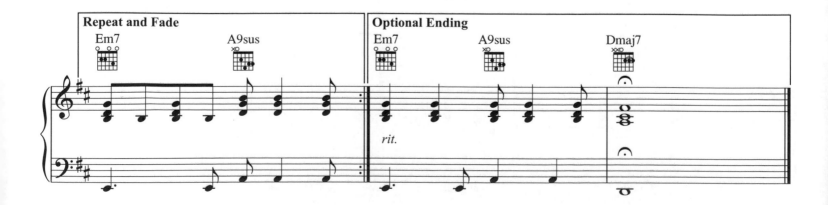

TIME AFTER TIME

Words and Music by CYNDI LAUPER
and ROB HYMAN

you can look__ and you will__ find me,__ time af - ter time.__

If you fall,__ I will catch__ you; I'll be____ wait - ing,__

To Coda 𝄌

1

time af - ter time.__

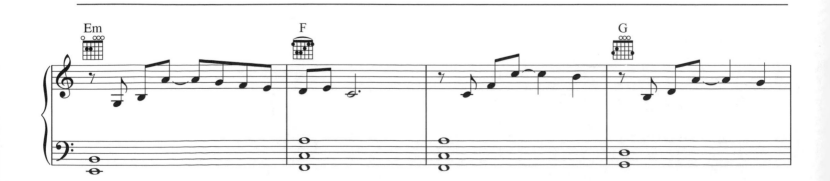

TAKE MY BREATH AWAY
(Love Theme)
from the Paramount Picture TOP GUN

Words and Music by GIORGIO MORODER
and TOM WHITLOCK

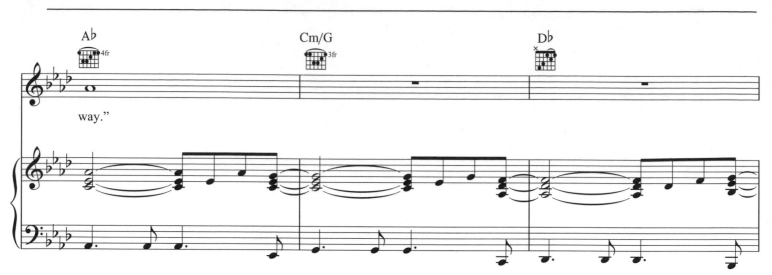

Through the hour-glass I saw ___ you. In time, ___ you slipped ___ a - way. ___

___ When the mir - ror crashed, I called ___ you and turned ___

watch-ing in slow __ mo - tion as you turn __ my way _____ and

Repeat and Fade

say, "Take my breath a - way,

Optional Ending

my love." __ "Take my breath a -

TINY DANCER

Words and Music by ELTON JOHN
and BERNIE TAUPIN

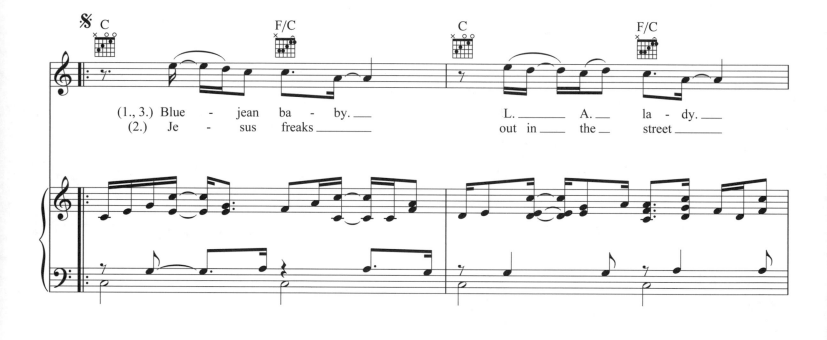

(1., 3.) Blue - jean ba - by. ___ L. ___ A. ___ la - dy. ___
(2.) Je - sus freaks _____ out in ___ the ___ street _____

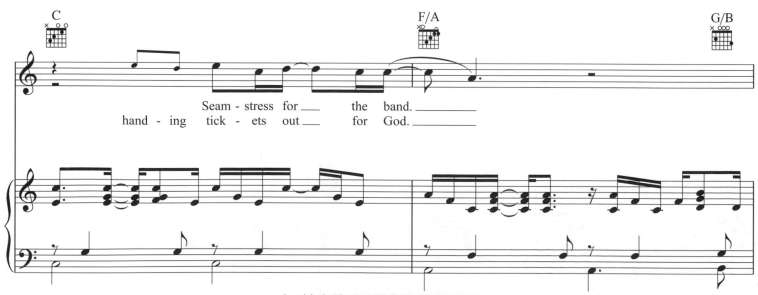

Seam - stress for ___ the band. _____
hand - ing tick - ets out ___ for God. _____

And now ___ she's in me, ___ al - ways ___ with me, ___ she sings the ___ songs. ___
Look - ing on, ___ ti - ny danc - er in my hand. ___
The word she ___ knows, the tune she hums. ___

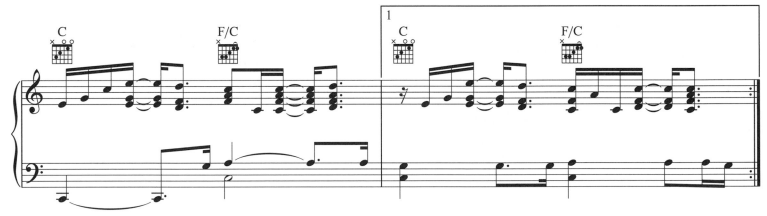

But, oh, how it feels ___ so real ___

way.   Lay me down   in sheets   of lin -

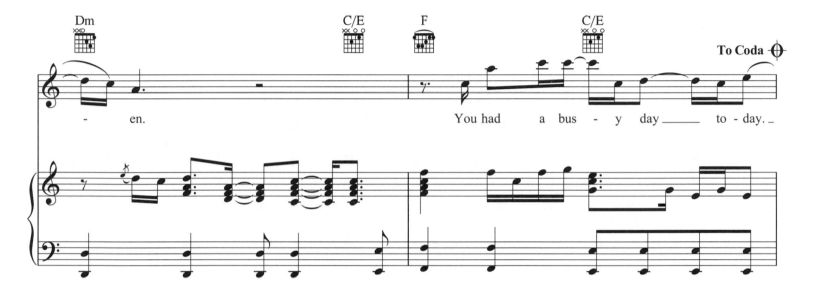

- en.   You had   a   bus - y day   to - day.

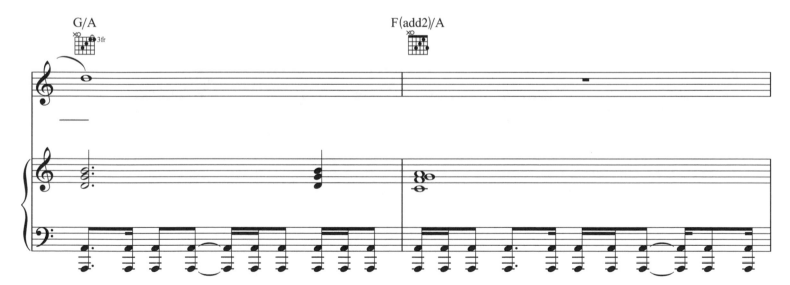

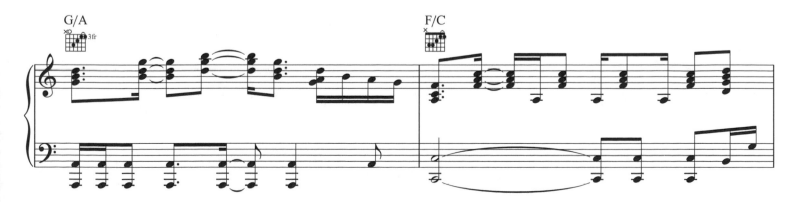

D.S. al Coda
(take 3rd ending)

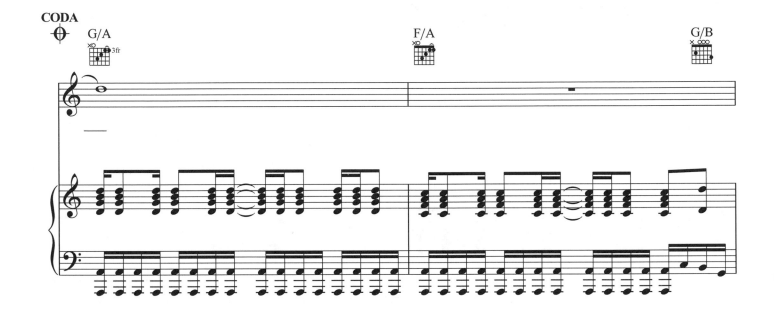

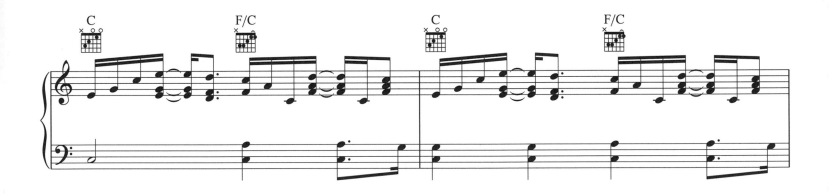

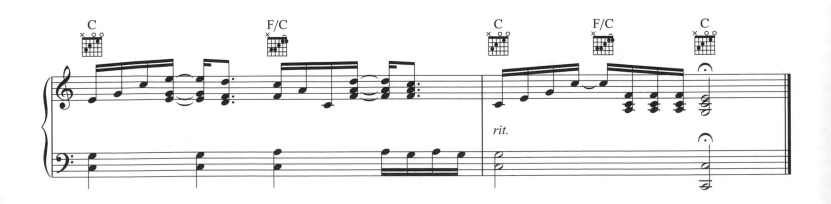

UP WHERE WE BELONG

from the Paramount Picture AN OFFICER AND A GENTLEMAN

Words by WILL JENNINGS
Music by BUFFY SAINTE-MARIE and JACK NITZSCHE

UN-BREAK MY HEART

Words and Music by
DIANE WARREN

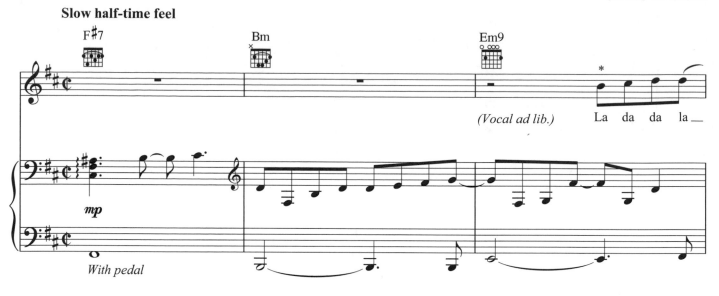

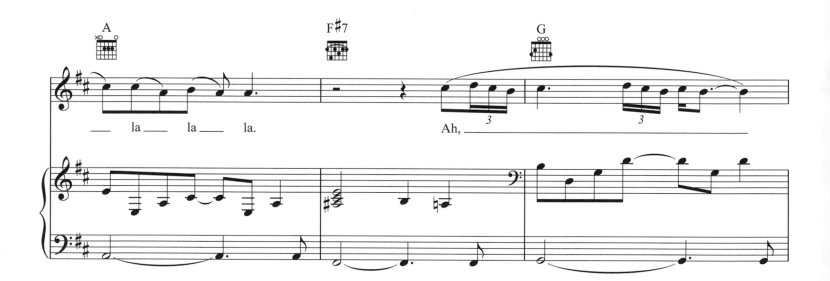

Vocal written octave higher than sung.

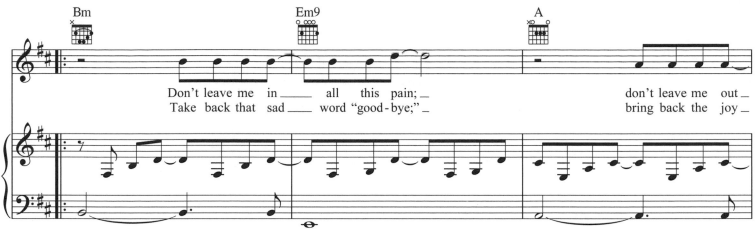

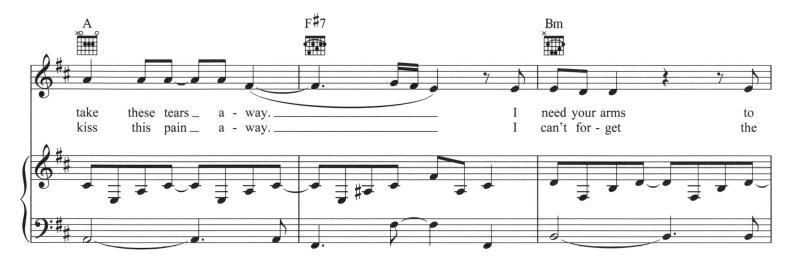

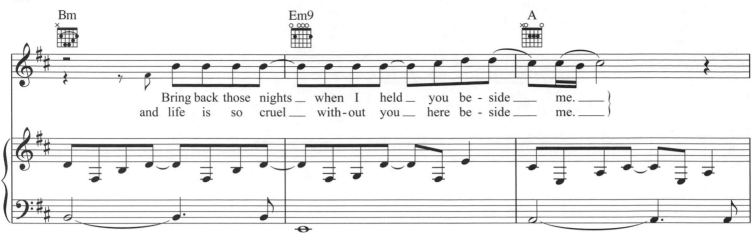

Bring back those nights ___ when I held ___ you be-side ___ me. ___
and life is so cruel ___ with-out you ___ here be-side ___ me. ___

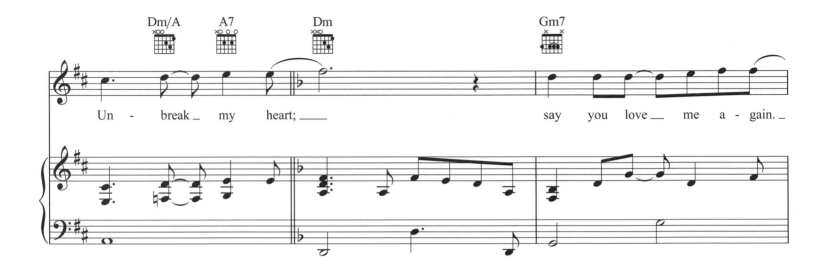

Un - break ___ my heart; ___ say you love ___ me a - gain. ___

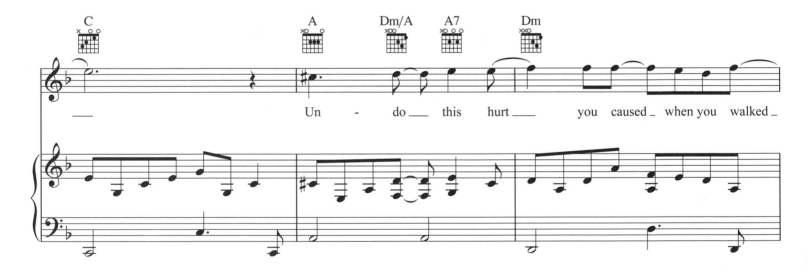

___ Un - do ___ this hurt ___ you caused ___ when you walked ___

___ out the door ___ and walked out ___ of my life. ___ Un - cry ___ these tears ___

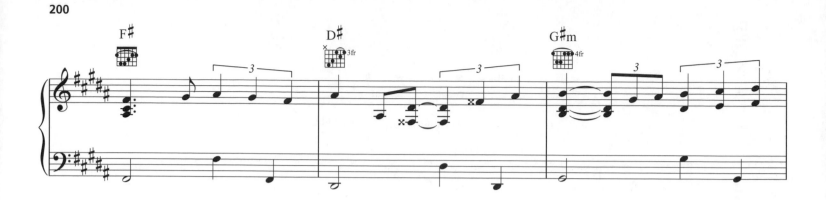

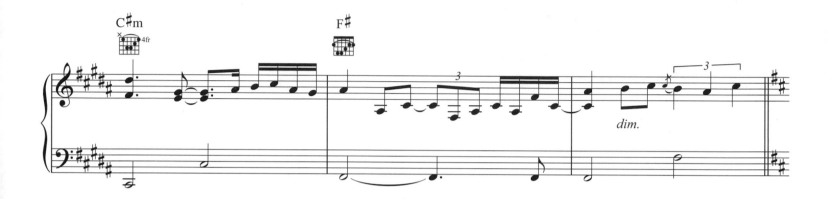

* Vocal written as sung

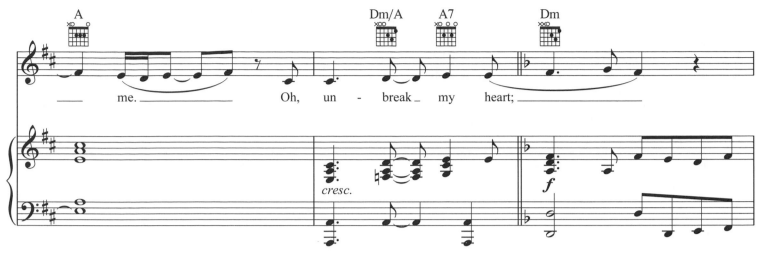

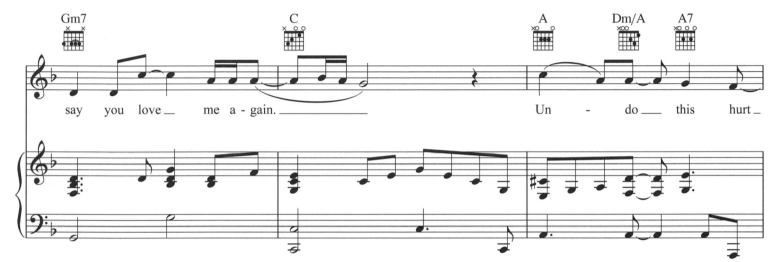

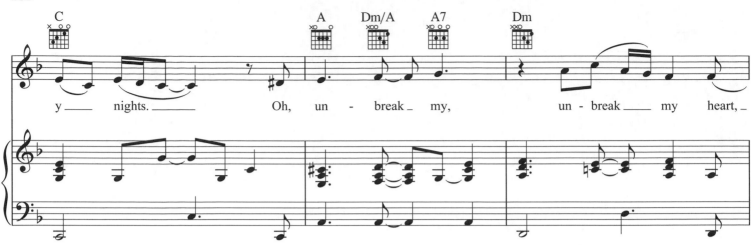

WONDERFUL TONIGHT

Words and Music by
ERIC CLAPTON

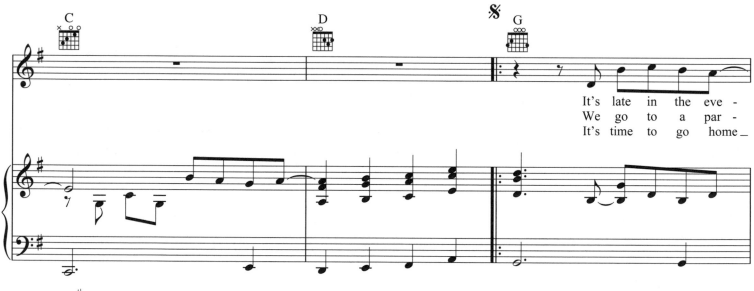

It's late in the eve -
We go to a par -
It's time to go home __

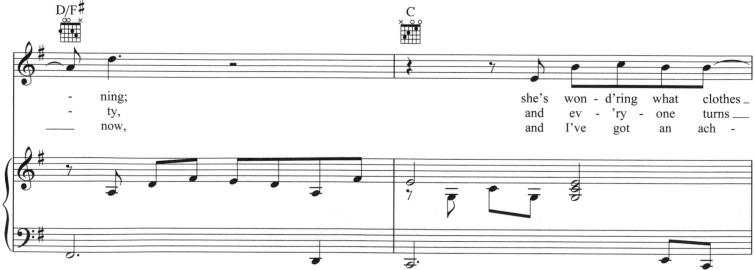

- ning;
- ty,
__ now,

she's won - d'ring what clothes __
and ev - 'ry - one turns __
and I've got an ach -

"Yes, you look won-der-ful _____ to-night." _____
"Yes, I feel won-der-ful _____ to-night." _
dar-ling, you are won-der-ful _____ to-night. _____

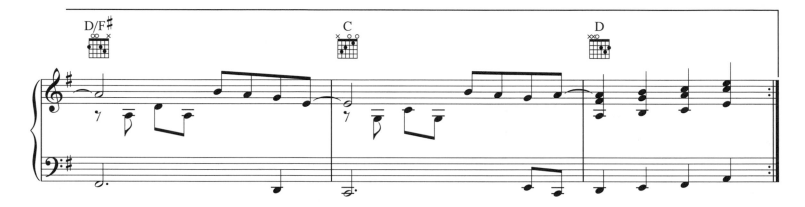

_____ I feel won-der-ful _____ be-

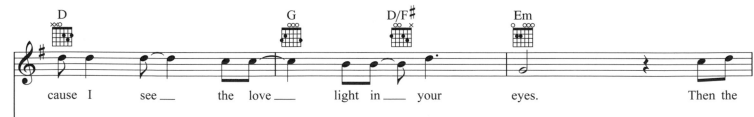

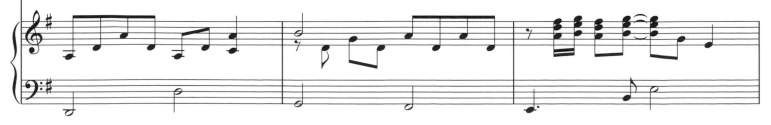

cause I see _____ the love _____ light in _____ your eyes. Then the

wonder of it all _____ is that you just don't_ re - al - ize_

_____ how much _____ I love _____ you.

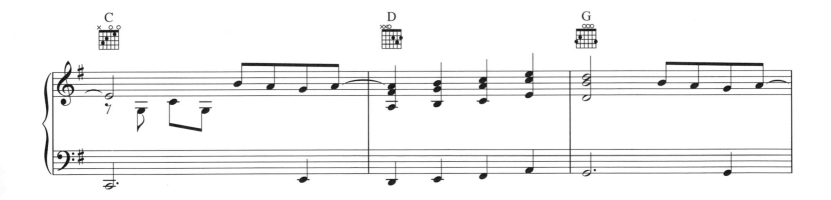

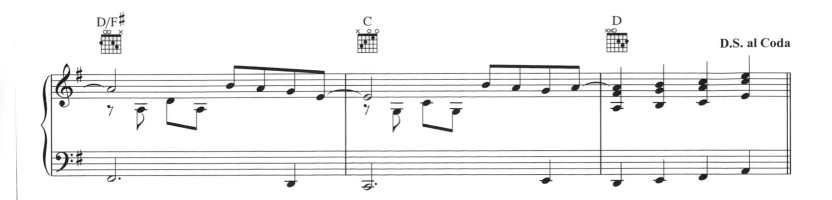

D.S. al Coda

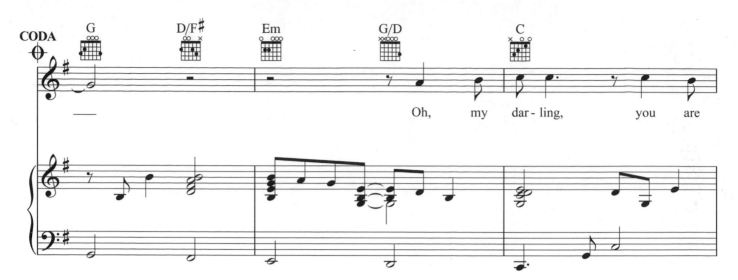

Oh, my dar - ling, you are

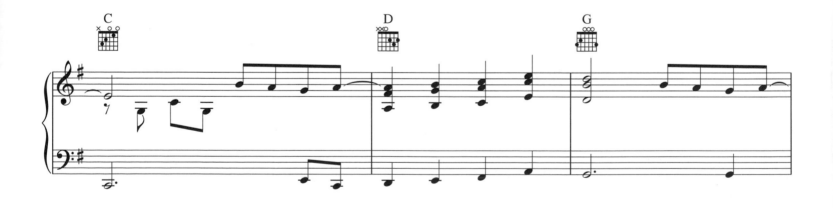

won-der - ful _____ to - night." _____

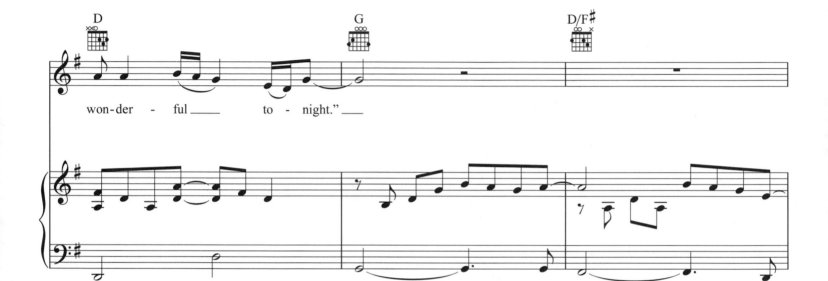

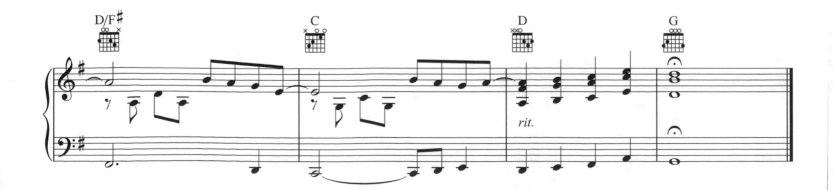